TRAVELS AND VOYAGES

TRAVELS AND VOYAGES

BETWEEN CALCUTTA AND INDEPENDENT TIPPERAH

SAMBHU C MOOKERJEE

GYAN

Published by

Gyan Publishing House
5, Ansari Road
Daryaganj, New Delhi-110002
Phone: 011-47034999, 9811692060
E-mail: books@gyanbooks.com

Distribution Network
gyanbooks.com
India, USA, Canada, UK, Australia

ISBN: 978-93-7097-873-7 (PB)

First Published, 1887

2nd Impression 2025

Printed at: Gyan Press, Delhi.

TRAVELS AND VOYAGES
Author: SAMBHU C MOOKERJEE

TRAVELS & VOYAGES

BETWEEN

CALCUTTA & INDEPENDENT TIPPERAH

BY

SAMBHU C. MOOKERJEE,

formerly Minister to His Highness the late
NAWAB FARIDOON JAH BAHADOOR,
(the last of the Nawabs Nazim of Bengal, Behar and Orissa,)
latterly Minister of His Highness
Maharaja Beer Chunder Dev Burmon Manikya Bahadoor,
of Independent Tipperah.

CALCUTTA:

REIS & RAYYET OFFICE.

1887.

"I know not how, in other lands,
The changing seasons come and go;
What splendours fall on Syrian sands,
What purple lights on Alpine snow!
Nor how the pomp of sunrise waits
On Venice at her watery gates;
A dream alone to me is Arno's vale,
And the Alhambra's halls are but a traveller's tale.

"Yet, on life's current, he who drifts
Is one with him who rows or sails;
And he who wanders widest lifts
No more of beauty's jealous veils
Than he who from his doorway sees
The miracle of flowers and trees,
Feels the warm Orient in the noonday air,
And from cloud minarets hears the sunset call to prayer!

"The eye may well be glad, that looks
Where Pharpar's fountains rise and fall;
But he who sees his native brooks
Laugh in the sun, has seen them all.
The marble palaces of Ind
Rise round him in the snow and wind;
From his lone sweetbrier Persian Hafiz smiles,
And Rome's cathedral awe is in his woodland aisles."

" The having spoken of myself with unaffected freedom will need little apology with the candid ; and let the uncandid consider that they injure me less than their own hearts and minds by misrepresentation. *Whatever talents a person may possess to amuse and instruct others, be they ever so inconsiderable, he is yet bound to exert them.*"

" Therefore should I
Be but the essence of deformity,
A coward, did my very eye-lids wink
At speaking out what I have dared to think."

TO

MY COUNTRYMEN, FIRST—

THOSE WHO KNOWING INDIA,

ARE YET UNABLE TO LOVE HER,—

OTHERS WHO, AS IN DUTY BOUND, LOVING,

KNOW HER NOT,—

OTHERS STILL WHO NEITHER KNOW NOR LOVE,—

THOSE AGAIN WHO REPAIR ABROAD FOR RECREATION

IN THE BELIEF THAT INDIA IS STALE, FLAT AND

UNPROFITABLE; NEXT,

TO FOREIGNERS WHO CARE TO KNOW;

AND, LAST NOT LEAST,

TO ENGLISHMEN,

ON WHOSE SYMPATHETIC KNOWLEDGE

DEPENDS THE GOOD OF THE INDIAN

MYRIADS;

IS RESPECTFULLY OFFERED, FOR CANDID USE,

THIS SAMPLE OF

A BOOK ON INDIA

BY AN INDIAN.

Calcutta, 1887.

CONTENTS.

JOURNEY FROM INDEPENDENT TIPPERAH IN 1881.

A CRUISE 'CROSS COUNTRY.

JOURNEY TO INDEPENDENT TIPPERAH IN 1884.

CALCUTTA TO DACCA.

THROUGH MANY WATERS.

IN THE HEART OF BENGAL PROPER.

THE END OF THE VOYAGE.

AT AGARTALA: GLIMPSES OF LIFE IN A HINDU STATE.

THE CHRISTIAN VILLAGE IN TIPPERAH.

A GLANCE AT THE HISTORY OF PORTUGUESE SETTLEMENT IN BENGAL AND OF THE INTRODUCTION OF ARTILLERY TO THE EAST.

LIFE AT AGARTALA *(Continued.)*

CURIOUS CUSTOMS.

LAST DAYS AT AGARTALA.

THE LAST RETURN.

A FEW NOTES ON THE GEOGRAPHY AND CARTOGRAPHY OF EAST BENGAL.

THE DHALESWARI FAIR.

RUINS OF RAMPAL, THE HINDU CAPITAL.

PREFACE.

THIS is a book of travels at home—the journeyings of a Calcutta Bengali in Bengal Proper. Called to office in Tipperah, I, for the first time, in 1878, saw East Bengal. Since then I have been several times all through the country to that State and back. Having kept notes of what struck me I am enabled to lay them before the public. I only hope that what I thought of sufficient interest may be deemed not unprofitable.

Out of eight journeys, in all, counting returns, —here are accounts of only four—two trips to Tipperah and two trips back. Under the head of "Through East Bengal," is related my second tour, in 1878. "A Cruise 'cross Country" records my return from the third journey. The last portion is the narrative of my final voyages, to and fro, as well as of my sojourn in Tipperah, in 1884.

These several accounts are mainly transcripts from my Diaries, written at the time, often during my progress. Though they have, in passing through the press, undergone polishing, here and there, and been, in a few cases, added to, they are substantially a record of impressions taken down at the very moment or soon after. Therein, they may be held to have some value.

The first of the accounts (from the beginning to page 29,) appeared in 1882 in *Reis and Rayyet* weekly newspaper, in the Doorga Pooja (Hindu Festival) Number. The second (p. 30 to p. 64) was published in two issues of the *Statesman* in 1884. About the same time, the third (p. 65 to p. 202), too, appeared in *Reis and Rayyet.* The remainder—more than a third of the book—appears now for the first time. This portion is perhaps the most important, embracing the extracts from my Journals of Agartala and of the last voyage back, which appear under the heads of "Glimpses of Life in a Hindoo State," "A Glance at the History of Portuguese Settlement in Bengal and of the introduction of Artillery to the East," "Curious Customs," "Notes on Geography and Cartography," "The Dhaleswari Fair," "The Ruins of Rampal, the Hindoo Capital," &c.

Notwithstanding the care taken by my lynx-eyed friend, Baboo Jogesh Chunder Dutt, (for whose loving aid in this and other literary undertakings my best prayers are due,) I shall not be surprised to hear that several errors have been found. I have chanced to light upon two in the page-headings, and four or five in the body. The former I have corrected in the table of Contents. The latter are less manageable, and have given me uneasiness out of all proportion to their significance. Is there a fatality that condemns letter-press in the East to the necessity of dragging along with it a more or less copious list of Errata? To avoid that disfigurement, I would rather dispose of in the preface matters ordinarily left to be treated departmentally and formally, under a Latin heading. I therefore take the liberty to note here that in p. 153, in the 4th line from the bottom, the word "craft" had better be altered to "vessel," and the word "that" in line 12, p. 160 be read "this."

"Heared" in p. 24 l. 12, and "Thratened," p. 280, l. 15, should, of course, be "heard" and "threatened," respectively. P. 95, l. 2, omit "we." Classical and foreign words and names naturally give us most trouble. Thus *glebe*, p. 23, should be *glebae*. Apelles has been misspelt with two p's, p. 257. Perhaps a more vexatious misprint occurs in p. 162, where, by the intrusion of an additional "the," Byron's famous apostrophe—

"Ye stars! which are the poetry of Heaven!"

has come to be unscannable.

With respect to a new word in p. 217, I have to explain that though the strict form should be "pariarocracy" or, shortly, "pariacracy," I prefer "pariocracy" for its resemblance to the well-known words in that termination as well as for its facility of pronunciation. The multiplicity of uniform vowel sounds has a disagreeable effect. In Sir John Phear's "Bhadracracy" the a's have different sounds.

I need scarcely say that the verse occurring in the book is not mine.

I see that, in hastily adopting, for the convenience of the mere English reader, Sir William Jones' poetical version of a celebrated passage in the Odes of Hafiz, I have missed the point of my reference. Having almost mechanically given Jones' lines, I afterwards found, to my horror, that the man of the law, who might be expected to be precise, had quietly swallowed up the dear mole—without exhibiting a facial contortion. The original is—

Agar án Turki Shirazi bedest áred dili mårá
Bekháli hinduish bakhsham Samarcand o Bokhará:

meaning—*If that (fair) Turk of Shiraz would accept my heart, for the dark mole on her cheek*

I would give Samarcand and Bokhara.

This little verse is transformed by Sir William Jones, one of the best translators of Oriental poetry, and a man of true literary feeling and no small share of poetic sensibility, into the following elaborate address—

Sweet maid, if thou wouldst charm my sight,
And bid these arms thy neck infold ;
That rosy cheek, that lily hand,
Would give thy poet more delight
Than all Bocara's vaunted gold,
Than all the gems of Samarcand.

That is all very well, but where is the mole? There seems, indeed, a conspiracy among English writers against that dear little landmark of the human face divine. The ode of Hafiz of which this verse is the opening, is the most famous of all that great Poet's works. It is not only on every lip in Asia, but is well-known to Europeans of education, specially Anglo-Indians, as a type of Eastern poesy, just as the *Tázá bá tázá* is known as a type of Eastern music. Many, accordingly, have been the attempts to render it in English. But they have one and all been unlucky. That the native charm of poesy is not to be preserved in another tongue, even in a metrical rendering, is not surprising. Here, the very substance is missed. By a consensus of antipathy, the best-complimented part of woman—the principal feature of beauty—has been burked by these rhyming Dryasdusts. We have caught the illustrious Sir William Jones in the act of pilfering the charming black thing —charming by contrast with a fair ground. And now let us see the ways of a later singer. The Poet of the *Sunyassee* "does"—with a vengeance—the same passage thus—

> If Sheeraz' Beauty would receive
> My heart, and bid my arms enfold
> Her lily neck, Oh ! then believe,
> More dear her dimpled smile I'd hold,
> Than Samarcand's, Bokhara's gold.*

The legal and judicial translator approves himself the better poet, but the man of science —the poet-chirurgeon's version is rather more to the purpose. He has indeed adopted his predecessor's aspiration that the damsel should bid his arms her neck infold—with the addition of a complimentary epithet to her neck, and the change of *i* into *e* in the last verb. There he stops, however ; he does not stray beyond into unnecessary verbiage. For all that, he fails.

* *The Sunyassee, an Eastern Tale, and other Poems.* By James Hutchinson, Esq., Surgeon, on the Bengal Establishment, Secretary to the Medical Board, &c. Calcutta, 1838, p. 210.

His superior sense of a translator's responsibility does not prevent him from suppressing the characteristic thought of his original. In fact, European translators seem by common consent to avoid the black mole as the—Black Death! They apparently think it very weak of Hafiz—whom thy probably regard as a hoary-headed Persian Swinburne, ever mooning about woman and wine—to be ready, if only figuratively, to sacrifice the greatest cities of Central Asia at the height of their splendour for a girl disfigured by a sooty tumour on her cheek. Europeans will be able to speak more positively on the point. All I can say is that if this is so, a change must have come over the spirit of Europe's "dream of fair women." In the time of Queen Anne, at any rate, Europe doated on the artificial patches which did duty for natural moles on beauty's cheeks.

The Introduction is, I confess, an afterthought. But a preliminary explanation seems called for, to help the reader to understand the precise character of the book, or even to follow satisfactorily the narrative and the reflections.

S. C. M.

1, Wellington Square,
Calcutta, *September 12, 1887.*

INTRODUCTION.

TIPPERAH is an ancient country beyond the Megna and the Brahmapootra. These rivers have ever been recognised as the Eastern boundary of antique as well as of historical India, and they are still regarded as the limit, on that side, of geographical, as distinguished from political, India. From time immemorial, this land was ruled by a race who trace their descent to the most illustrious names in Indo-Aryan memory—the Heroes of Indraprastha immortalised by the Bards of the Mahabharata. The family—the Tipperah branch, that is—yet exist, clinging to a throne which is literally worshipped to this day, but shorn of power and the best part of their old possessions, and even divorced from their former capital. At one time, their will was law over all the territory between the Brahmapootra and Burma, West to East, and from the borders of Assam in the North to the Northern boundaries of Arracan in the South. At this day, they are confined within a small tract of low-hilly and generally forest country, having its capital on its Western fringe. Six hundred and seventy years ago, Tipperah arrested the wave of conquering Islam, and even disputed with the Moslem advance-guard the possession of the Eastern parts of CisMegnaic Bengal. The Persian historians of the Pathan Period record many wars between the Kings of Gour and the Rajas of Tipperah, in which sometimes the one side and at others the other side were worsted. The Annals of the Tipperah Race are naturally partial to national glory. For, Tipperah shares with Cashmere the distinction of possessing a written history. In our time, a "Baboo" bullies the representative of Yayati, the primeval Conqueror of the Lunar Race.

Old Tipperah is now politically split into two

—a British District and a Native Principality. British Tipperah, whose chief town and official head-quarters is Comillah, consists of the cultivated, fruitful and populous plains on the left of the Megna river. Independent Tipperah is the backwoods farther East, sparsely peopled, the home of many barbarous tribes, but of splendid promise in the near future, and teeming with historic associations and objects of scientific interest. It is now the official foible to call it Hill Tipperah, but that is a new-fangled misnomer—the so-called "hills" being mere mounds of earth for the most part, of no height. The local as well as popular Indian and, therefore, the true name, is Independent Tipperah.

In 1877, I was invited to office in Independent Tipperah. I remained there a few months, and then came away, to return in January next. After a stay of nearly two years at Agartala, I came back to Calcutta in 1879. In a few months, I again went for the third time in 1880, returning at the end of twenty-two months in 1881.

In 1884, an officer of the position of an acting Deputy Collector in the State, was deputed to Calcutta to fetch me up without fail, leaving me no option to doubt the Maharaja Bahadoor's earnestness or the urgency of the situation. The officer chosen for the duty, too, was a friend—the only connection of mine whom I had introduced to the Maharaja's service. I felt that I could not disappoint His Highness without compromising his envoy. Unfortunately, my avocations did not at the time permit of my leaving Calcutta. I was then pressed to come for a short time, after which I might return to Calcutta and act from there, repairing again to the scene when I could and considered it necessary. It was impossible to resist my kind old master, the more so for my genuine interest in the little kingdom. I had a great affection for Tipperah, deepened into pity by disappointment at having been unable to serve it to the extent of my intentions or capacity, so as to realize in it my ideal of a model Oriental State of the Nineteenth Century. Accordingly, I took advantage of the Long Vacation to go for a couple of months. I was detained much longer—beyond indeed the margin I had secretly reserved in my mind. I received the most pressing reminders from my colleagues and constituents at Calcutta. Nevertheless, I could not come away in less than six months. This was my last visit, and my fourth residence in Tipperah. I left Calcutta in the middle of July and returned on Christmas-day.

This little booklet is the record of some of my journeys forwards and backwards, and of some incidents of my last sojourn in the Principality.

THROUGH EAST BENGAL.

IT was with the odour of New Year's Day festivities still on me that I proceeded to my work in the far East. This was my second cut through the heart of Bengal Proper to the extreme frontier on that side. The first step was to book myself for the mail to Dacca, and start. After the night passage by rail, I embarked on board the steam-boat at Goalundo. I had great difficulty in finding accommodation, we were so many on board. Luckily for me, warned by previous experience, I had reserved my cabin by telegraph. It was not without some degree of tranquil satisfaction, though without any unworthy enjoyment, that I saw my housing secured, while so many as good as myself, nay, better perhaps—all of them being Whites—were roaming about the decks, above and below, before and behind, in search of a home. Some of them seemed to knock against my door continually, as if not realising the fact of the occupation—perhaps unable to realise the possibility of the Heathen black being comfortably quartered on a steamer in an Indian river in British Territory while yet a single European was reduced to the *rôle* of the Wandering Jew! Once or twice I discerned danger in the air, but courage and luck carried me safe through it. For, though the Company might put me in possession—to maintain it against a determined British invader more mindful of his own comfort than punctilious about the means of attaining it, was not easy. Matters, however, did not come to that extremity. A bold front scared trespassers away. But the peril to which my castle on board was exposed, heightened my appreciation of my advantage. I could not but feel grateful to Providence and, after and under It, the British Government. Nor could I help feeling for those of my fellow-passengers who were constrained in that mid-winter to voyage through the great river without cabin accommodation. It was with real distress that I saw so many, stowed away at night in all sorts of places, likely and unlikely, on board. For this was one of the heaviest invasions on the line. The fact is, it was the "season," and gentlemen and jockeys, men and beasts, were hurrying forward to Dacca for the races.

Among the gentlemen I met were the District Superintendent of Dacca, a lean, agile man, and apparently no fool in his profession ; the Principal of the College, a grave venerable man who stares you through his massive dark blue spectacles completely protecting the eyes—or rather one of them, for the gentleman had lost the other—who was about proceeding on furlough to Europe by way of the Pacific Railway ; his successor, a short young Scotchman, son of a well-known Southern Missionary ; another whiskered "brither Scot" of almost monumental height —who might have been a *sizar* at the University of Brobdignag, but whose size may strike terror into the hearts of his puny pupils of Bengal —who professes mathematics—the giant that is, not the pupils; and a Colonel who must be well-known on the turf, who was naturally the heartiest and best mannered of them all. He played whist with our commander at the latter's quarters, and they endured a Baboo watching the game. Another Colonel was not anything so kind, although the churl had the best of reasons in the world for being at peace with mankind, including blues, blacks, buffs, bays, roans, iron-greys, olives, and all. He held a fine sinecure as commanding at Dacca—in the centre of an unmartial population—and he had just married a fair wife who was also on board. For once, however, Beauty was clearly beaten by the unconscionable—Bull.

And beauty draws us by a single hair

proved a miserable fable, when the presence and

propinquity of the goddess fully equipped, failed to moderate the scowl of Apis. So far as its humanising influence goes,

> The might—the majesty of loveliness

was simply wasted on his godship. It seemed as if he thought

> beauty stands
> In the admiration only of weak minds
> Led captive.

We had no singing on board, nor instruments to play upon, but judging by analogy I verily believe either would have been unavailing. The sublimest and most effective of the Fine Arts would, I am afraid, have been disgraced in the vain effort to conciliate this son of Mars. Music can soothe the savage breast ; it maddens the languishing-eyed gazelle for joy ; it draws the coiled serpent out of its hole ; it may possibly soften rocks or bend the knotted oak : I would have liked to see it try its trick upon the enlightened heart of the military Briton !

Whether musing by himself or supporting the pretty angel on his arm, he was the victim of low spirits. He was not in good health, in fact. He suffered always from one disease at any rate —opthalmia, of an obstinate type; and the cause was ever the same—the Baboo. He and I were near betraying our mutual relations to the whole vessel. Luckily it was a matter of little over 24 hours. We soon came to our journey's end. The following morning we reached Naraingunge, and a few hours later, Dacca.

At Dacca I took, for my voyage further East, one of the fine roomy green country barges locally called *Kose*, besides smaller homely craft for kitchen and servants. I travelled in some state, with two friends for companions and a small troop of attendants and guards. In spite of all conveniences, however, it was an inexpressibly tedious trip. The great galley moved at a snail's pace. The change from railway and steamer made it a positive torture.

Leaving Dacca, we stopped for the night at

Futoolla. Thence we made the angle of the Booriganga. Passing into the Dhaleswari, we drifted down, past the mouth of the Lakhya, past the confluence of the old, almost dried up, Brahmaputra—the legitimate Eastern boundary of ancient Bengal and the Aryan Pale. We wound round into the channel of the Megna, named in the Surveyor-General's map Nowadee River, and stemming the stream up, passed into the Megna proper and, after dark, stopped off Baidyabazar.

1878, January 12, Saturday.—At dawn left our mooring near Baidyabazar. A cloudy and rather foggy morning. Yesterday we had observed the phenomenon of boats literally *sailing* up and down the Megna,—the wind being, I suppose, so equivocal—at the confluence of the Dhaleswari and the Megna. Further up, the wind, if it deserved the name, was with us. To-day, it is decidedly against, blowing from the North. Of course, the morning is pleasantly cool.

This morning, we slowly proceeded up the great river. Making the curve of the Megna, we entered the narrow channel named in the map Nya Kharee—which passes through the vast alluvial deposit *(chur)* formed along the left bank of the main stream and fronting Pargana Maheshurdee,—and, passing Jawakandee, Beebeerkandee, and Sonakandee, again found ourselves in the main Megna, and remained at night somewhere off Sonarampur.

To a Bengali travelling on business, it may be said there can hardly be very much of interest in a passage through the rivers of his own country. But in point of fact, the observing eye will always find something worth seeing or even dwelling upon, something, perchance, to treasure up and remember. It is specially interesting for the native to mark the varieties of man and society as he glances past the villages of his country, along the water ways, hundred after hundred, riding after riding and shire after shire. This morning, at any rate, we were struck by the appearance of a whole *ghatful* of Mahomedan lasses and old dames all bathing in front of their houses on the bank. None of them were fair, or had been ; even that Indian yellow, which is at such a discount with Thackeray, was nowhere. They are but the homely wives and daughters of the poor Islamite cultivators, stupidly scorned by their inferiors as the *Shavenheads*—and yet what tidiness, what show of comfort, not without a fair share of elegance, in their ample, substantial, colored striped robes, what grace and sprightliness joined to all necessary femininity in the balanced shapely forms, and their deportment! They were all fine healthy girls, with well-proportioned, nimble limbs. A couple of them were sitting at the edge of the water elaborately scrubbing and towelling their persons, and helping to clean one another. I admired their modest yet unflurried demeanour no less than the skill and resolution and withal simple dignity with which they went through the operation, without, for a moment, exposing any part of their flesh on which the eye of strangers should never fall. I was reminded of the similar skill I had remarked in the Maharatta and Nagar women in the *ghats* of Benares. One of the two girls was not without a kind of attraction in her plump person and rather olive complexion and her large black eyes, though the face is forbidding, with an owlish expression. There was another damsel darker than most yet more inviting than all, with copious curled black hair, drawn together and tied behind her head in a Grecian knot. And she had such large languishing eyes! The bodice or jacket that fitted her fine person made her the more interesting in my eyes—exhibiting her as a being of refinement superior to the Hindu damsels in her position in life. The jewels, or apologies for jewels, on her person, were rude enough. But, then, she was not doomed to the distress of comparison. The taste of the people seemed simple as their knowledge is confined. Few in number and plain as was the aggregate of all the ornature, of different kinds, sported by the village woman-kind, the trinkets and gewgaws were sufficient for vanity on one side and envy on another.

About 9 in the morning we touched at a village on our left (as we go up the Megna) called Sonargaon Bardi. We purchased fish and cleaned the cooking utensils and plates in the sands of the beach. As I lay watching languidly the latter operation, tedious as it ever is, my attention was whipped up by the appearance of a fine healthy girl with a fairish olive complexion and mass of black hair and, of course, black eyes, come to fetch water from the stream. From the linen jacket she wore, she is a Mahomedan. It was interesting, though by no means singular, to see here as elsewhere the Mussulmans—though here they were all of the agricultural classes—distinguished from their Hindu neighbours by their living, their breeding, their vivacity.

The maid of Sonargaon might be welcomed

in a harem. With her rich hair flowing down behind, or floating about like a streamer in the air, it was a joy indeed to see her carry her easy burden of water. She almost ran with the vessel on her hip! Such graceful curves her figure presented in that position as the eye of artist might dwell upon for ever!

The most surprising anthropological curiosity that I ever saw was in a young woman—from the condition of her still fine bust she might have passed but once through the hands of the village *accoucher*—a Mussulmani again—who had utilized her Derbyshire neck into an advantage, by adorning it with an elaborate necklace to match, almost veiling the whole fleshy ridge. One could with difficulty refrain from laughter. For all that, we admired the ingenuity displayed. I don't know whether it is a common device in these parts. The tumour is more prevalent in Mymensing, and particularly in Assam—in the latter Province attacking mostly those who use tank water. This is the first case of such swelling we have met with in our journey in the Dacca country, and it must be admitted that the sufferer, if so she may be called, has put the best face upon the matter. For the time being at any rate, this thing of ill omen has been converted into a thing of beauty, if not a joy for ever. The device is a curious evidence of adaptability. The taste and judgment of the thing was obvious. It certainly looked elegant. With a little habit we may imagine Assam gallant addressing sonnets to the additional neck of his sweetheart. A Baruah bard may yet immortalise the goitre under beauty's chin, even as Hafiz has immortalised the mole on beauty's cheek.

> Sweet maid, if thou wouldst charm my sight,
> And bid these arms thy neck infold ;
> That rosy cheek, that lily hand,
> Would give thy poet more delight
> Than all Bocara's vaunted gold,
> Than all the gems of Samarcand.

Of course, all art would have been wasted without proper material to work upon. But

Nature, kind even in severity, relented in the very act her dire visitation upon the poor victim. In punishing her with the goitre she has given her no unmanageable burden to carry through life—no hideous heap of an addition to the body. This girl's superfluous flesh is no obstructive or obtrusive thing but a gentle swelling rising evenly from the sides and terminating in a modest knob, at the centre.

I am infinitely delighted to observe the evidences of comfort and comparative civilization in the peasantry of these parts. It is something that so many about here are well protected in this cold weather by the cheap cottons and woollens of Europe. The women have all more costly ornaments, if less heavy and numerous, than their mothers or grand-mothers could boast of. We rarely come across the old abomination of the twisted legcuff, *(bànk mal)* as it deserves to be called rather than anklet. Shell bracelets are few and far between, but of a more manageable description than the manacles used of yore.

Silver clearly predominates. Brass is nowhere. At Dacca, we saw the Hindustani women had replaced by smaller and lighter silver jewellery their heavy pewter bracelets. Here, on the banks of the Megna, we found all the women display silver, some in profusion. It was all due to Jute.

January 13, Sunday.—This morning we entered the smaller channel of the Megna to the right, passed Maniknagar (near Shamgaon). Soon the bank on our right in the British frontier District of Tipperah rises to several feet, giving us a foretaste of the nature of the ground in the farther East. At one place there has been a landslip from the encroachment of the river As we made a momentary halt, to purchase fish from a solitary fisher-woman, who gave the name of the place as something like "Larabara," I had an opportunity of making a closer inspection. The height of the site of the landslip cannot be less than 8 or 9 cubits above the water. The slip has exposed the whole soil to that depth. It is not the usual alluvial deposit characteristic of the soil of these parts, as, indeed, of the whole Delta. Almost the first layer from the surface is some two or three feet of oxide of iron-tinged earth, at places showing a dirty golden hue, next comes the darker sand mixture known in our Calcutta district as *Gangamritika* or "Ganges earth," and lastly a blacker would-be loam.

January 14, Monday. At 8 O'clock last evening, we reached Gokarna—Gopon, the commander persists in calling it—where we anchored for the night. It was a chilly afternoon and evening, in consequence of a gentle breeze. The poor Baboo "for all his feathers, was a-cold." Nevertheless, I was determined to come out of my dormitory into the open deck to converse, according to my wont, with the boatmen and enquire about the villages on the banks, and so I buckled myself up for the enterprise by encasing my shivering person in thick loose trousers over our national robe (*dhoti*) wound up tight and woollen stockings and, for the upper limbs, a pair of coats, great and small, over a flannel shirt. Still it would not do, and after an hour's perseverance I gave up the struggle, and retired into my bed-room.

Oh paradox of human passion! there is pride of pedigree even in the Pariah! There is Koolinism even among the Chandals—for so our sailors are, under their Sanskritish designation of *namasudra*. Most of the young fellows are unmarried. With them, no less than with their betters, marriage is an expensive luxury. They have to pay a premium of from Rs. 50 at the lowest up to Rs. 150 (£6 to £18) for each bride besides giving five treats—now rice and curries, again *chura* and *dahi*, and so on,—to their castemen to the number of 150 or thereabouts. Altogether a wedding cannot be effected under less than Rs. 150; it usually comes up to Rs. 250. The higher the pedigree of the girl, the higher the premium. I suggested that they might be working for their marriage. It was true enough; they hardly cared to deny the soft impeachment. Nevertheless, they all complained that marriage was their ruin. They usually run into comparatively heavy debt on the occasion, and are hardly ever out of it. There is some exaggeration, doubtless. For, all said, these watermen are a prosperous set. There are many signs of this. Their bearing itself shews it. Their mode of spending their leisure demonstrates it. One of the purest consolations of riverine travel in Bengal is to watch these brave pariahs, emancipated by the slow but sure operation of economic causes, with a light heart at work at the oar or on the tow-rope during the day, and asking no man's permission to make merry in the evening, singing in concert and playing on the instruments, till a late hour sometimes. They certainly did not ask mine, though I am known to be somebody, the Rajbari with which I am connected being in great reputation in this part of the country, and the best customer of these barges. There might be some difficulty, with European passengers without an ear for music, who might regard such attempt at amusement in their presence an impertinence. Happily Europeans are not all of the same kidney, and a high member of the Bengal Education Department, Mr. C. B. Clarke, has left on record his ingenuous appreciation of the music of the *manjees*.

There is something in the life of the sailor—the monotone of its toil, or its alternation of hard exertion, at times violent and anxious, with dead-calm listless leisure—that disposes him to song as a suitable relief. Whatever may be the case in the frigid North, this is true of the warm South. Every "sentimental traveller," every student of literature, will recall the gondolier. The boatmen of Bengal's partiality is well-known. Grave historians love to tell how no native craft, small or large, ever rounded the fort of Monghyr without the sailors paying their homage of song to the memory of the great Jagat Seth and his brother hurled to death from its tower by the ruthless Nawab Nazim, and, above all, to that of the Seths' heroic valet, Choonnee, who pressed the offer of his own life to save his masters. The singing may be true to this day, though its subject must be different, for I am sure the historians, as in so many other cases, have perpetrated and perpetuated a fable. Nor are all classes of our sailors equally addicted to, or at least well up in, this rational recreation. The Hindus carry off the palm, being most devoted and most proficient. But only the Bengali Hindus. The upcountry navigators are an obviously lower type of animals. Even the Bengali Mussulmans are no good. But of all Bengali Hindu sailors, the Eastern boatmen are the most advanced. Nor is this inconsistent with Indian sociology in general, any more than with Hindu belief. The ancient legists reserve the profession of music for the mixed orders and the lowest classes, and to this day the despised Dom and Dhadi practise it. No wonder, therefore, to see such love of sweet sounds among the lowly!

Accordingly, these Chandals excel most in music. These Eastern sailors of all Indian mariners, from ferrymen and wherrymen to *lascars*, or, indeed, of any others of the humbler classes, habitually enjoy their own concerts, vocal and instrumental. Well might Mr. Clarke speak rapturously of this music as the sweetest indigenous sort. That is a characteristic European opinion, though. Europeans, indeed, have no opportunity of acquainting themselves with the true Oriental art. In discussing the subject they can never get over the *tom tom.* But though neither the singing nor the accompaniment has any pretensions to science or superior cultivation, the free concerts to which the passenger on board the Dacca barges are treated, are good enough, and occasionally excellent of their kind ; and heard under favorable conditions, on the bosom of our great rivers, the plaintive notes, carried by the breeze to the ear of the sleepy or sleeping European, dreaming of far off home beyond the main, might even charm. It must be the famous Dacca knights of the oar that inspired our Indian minstrel, provoking the Bengali into English verse in

THE BOATMEN'S SONG TO GANGA.

Gold river! gold river! how gallantly now
Our bark on thy bright breast is lifting her prow,
In the pride of her heauty, how swiftly she flies:
Like a white-winged spirit thro' topaz-paved skies.

Gold river! gold river! thy bosom is calm,
And o'er thee, the breezes are shedding their balm:
And Nature beholds her fair features pourtrayed,
In the glass of thy bosom—serenely displayed.

Gold river! gold river! the sun to thy waves,
Is fleeting to rest in thy cool coral caves;
And thence, with his tiar of light, at the morn
He will rise, and the skies with his glory adorn.

Gold river! gold river! how bright is the beam,
Which brightens and crimsons thy soft flowing stream;
Whose waters beneath make a musical clashing,
Whose ripples like dimples in childhood are flashing.

Gold river ! gold river ! the moon will soon grace
The hall of the stars with her light-shedding face :
The wandering planets her palace will throng,
And seraphs will waken their music and song.

Gold river ! gold river ! our brief course is done,
And safe in the city our home we have won ;
And now as the bright sun who drops from our view,
So Ganga, we bid thee a cheerful adieu ! *

Blessed be the Bengali boatman ! Blessed in especial the gondolier of our Eastern Venice !

Our Chandals have thriven, whoever else may have decayed under British rule. They are not the *adstricti glebe* of old—they are no more outcastes. Predial bondage being passed, they are enjoying the new sensation of looking men—the other and superior classes—in the face. Social progress goes hand in hand with material advancement, and moral regeneration follows material improvement. The

* *The Shair and Other Poems.* By Kashiprasad Ghosh. Calcutta. This was the first English verse published by a pure native Indian. Babu Kashiprasad Ghosh was otherwise a distinguished man of his time.

change, of late years, in the economic position and prospects of these once degraded people has gradually led to a social revolution. To begin with, they have altered their tribal designation. They probably resent being called by the notorious, and ominous term "Chandal." Are they not Namasudras? In fine, they have ceased to regard themselves the despised set they had been; and they have caused themselves to be taken at much their own valuation. They go the length of dictating to their social gods. My companion Ananda Babu heared at Moorshedabad that they now refuse to eat of the leavings of the superior castes below the Brahmans. Their living, though it may have improved, does not appear to the casual visitor from the metropolis to have done so. At any rate, they have a sufficiency of rice and fish and pulse, and that is as much as most Bengalis of the humbler ranks care for, and what many do not get. They don't mind running to a village and running off with an ordinary-sized pumpkin, laying down 3 pice, (about 3 farthings,) without a moment's haggling. This is secretly resented by the struggling *Bhadracracy** as the pursepride of the prosperous *cannaile.* Fifty years back, these very sailors would have given their life's blood rather than parted with a single copper coin. Even the superior classes could scarcely afford to pay so much as 3 farthings for a small gourd, and would certainly have regarded the demand absurdly extravagant. The pecuniary *insouciance* of our boatmen, however, is only another of the signs of the economic transition through which the country is passing. Our crew take two meals of rice in twenty four hours, consuming 15lb. (4+3½ seer) of rice morning and evening, between 9 persons. They do not generally have *dal* (pulse) twice a day. They

* A useful coin of the mint of one of our best judges (Sir John B. Phear) and ought to be adopted, were it only in his memory. The word was needed, however. There is no English equivalent for *Bhadra-lok*—the respectable people, or civilised men. The old *Aryans* were the earliest *Bhadracracy* in India.

live well in the sense of using a sufficiency of oil and salt and other spices and taking lots of fish. Formerly they could not afford the luxury of condiments to that extent. Even now, like other Bengalis', their diet is innocent of all butter, melted or unmelted. We could with difficulty, after days of research, get tolerable *ghee* (melted butter) at Dacca—a capital city and a seat of pillaw-eaters. Our Muktear there represented to us, and he ought to know, that the inhabitants hardly use any ghee in their food. Any little of it they do use in the way of condiment is supplied from the stinking vessels of the common hawkers with their execrable stuff. The Mussulmans too, those even of the middle classes, according to him, are no better. I can hardly credit this. I know Mahomedans. They cannot be so far gone even so far East. I suppose Muktear Saheb was ashamed, and, mindful of the honor of his fishy Eastern Hindus, ran the Mussulmans down to *their* disgrace. Indeed, the existence of the itinerant vendor of the stink called ghee goes to prove that ghee cannot be so unknown, though the consumption is, of course, confined to the Mussulmans. My opinion, however, is that it is better to be without butter in any form than be poisoned by the stuff so sold. I only hope the stuff sold in Dacca is far more innocent than the hideous Calcutta composition.

We have had plenty of fish during the voyage —too much of it—in compensation for the dearth we suffered from in June last, in our first trip to Tipperah. *Then* we had fish one day in three, perhaps. Not that there was any absence of fish in the river, but none could be got to purchase. Few fishers could be induced to approach our river man-of-war. These great boats are looked upon with suspicion by the people about here as carrying "big wigs"— Sahebs and their oppressive servants. Perhaps, too, fish were less abundant than in this cold season. Sometimes, as in the last voyage, we got Hilsa, two of which were purchased for us for two pice, on the second day. The first day we had to content ourselves with little shrimps. On the third day we had *hilsa* and *koi* and *phesa*. To-day we have purchased *chingri*, *nados*, *kharsola*, *tengra*, *pona*, &c., and this is our last day on board. Our pot is already on the fire with *khichri*, we meaning to have our breakfast before we reach Mugra, where there might be lots of people to come and see us, who had better not surprise the twice-born at the occult operation of cooking and eating on board. As there is no knowing when, if at all, we shall have another opportunity to-day of tasting cooked victuals, we should take as good a meal as the circumstances allow. For a substantial savoury repast at short notice, commend me to the Indian *olla podrida*—the *khichri* !

But we do not reach Mugra, after all, thanks to this most tortuous stream the Teetas !

15*th January, Tuesday.*—Leaving Gokarna yesterday early in the morning, we *gooned* up to Bonguz, a village on the left bank of the Teetas belonging to the Maharaja's Estate. The boat would no further go, for love or for money. There is no water. It is piteous to behold the desperate efforts of the crews of other boats to go up or come down. Only the small craft, with such light cargo as native pottery, can at all hope to move, and they are being pulled through the bed of the stream by the men almost knee-deep in mud.

16*th*, *Wednesday*.—From Bonguz a few hours' journey by land brings us to Agartala.

A CRUISE 'CROSS COUNTRY.

Notes of a Journey from Independent Tipperah in 1881.

September 22, 1881.—Bound for home, sweet home! By continuous hard and responsible work night and morning, noon and evening, I have more than earned my right to some respite. Others, both high and low, go home regularly every Doorga Pooja, and do not think of coming back till after *all* the Poojas and festivals. They are entitled, by regulation, to a month's leave in every twelve-month, but, by petition from home, they may easily get any extension, and, petition or no petition, nobody suffers by keeping himself away any length of time, the lapse being invariably pardoned. In this, as in other matters, native rulers are exceedingly liberal, and the old traditions are still thoroughly maintained in Tipperah. For all that, *I* cannot avail myself to the full of the advantages of the place, in the manner of the rest. My home is more distant. My journey to and fro is too expensive, from the state imposed upon me by my position in the durbar, for frequent repetition. Above all, my office cannot well be put in commission, so that I have got to look after affairs as far as practicable, wherever I may be. Accordingly, neither am I disposed, nor permitted by master or circumstances, to run away from Court, at the risk of causing something of an interregnum, so to say. But even functionaries in native States are but men, and though they might forego rest or recreation, they must occasionally attend to their private affairs, and families, and visit their own far away castles. After confining me for some two years within the hills, the Maharaja Bahadoor could not well refuse to set me at large. But though I got permission to go home, between one thing and another, I found it difficult to get away. His Highness himself, in his easy, indifferent way, withheld the final word. Perhaps it was rational instinct, rather than indifference. I was detained on this or that trumpery plea, but so long as I remained at the capital there was always business of a more or less important sort to attend to. I call at the *Rajbari* to tender my parting blessing (as son of Brahma sprung from the divine mouth), I take leave of the sons, but the father is not to be thus "done." His Highness knows that my barge from Dacca has not yet arrived. If the barge is in sight, it is not yet at the landing. If the vessel is at anchor in port, the cargo is yet on shore. Thus from day to day, finally from morn to noon, from noon to dewy eve, and again the following morning, from an amiable inability to make up the mind—a generous indisposition to part! Far from unpleasant is this dilly-dally, where there is no urgency, no peremptory call to promptitude. British employés know not this "unbought grace of life." They will probably not appreciate it. They have not the happiness of serving men, but are mere parts of a machine. *We* serve flesh and blood. The position of officials in native States has its disadvantages; many enough, to be sure; but it is not without ample compensations, and *this* is one of them.

The longest night, however, will become day, and I was allowed to say my effectual "good-bye." It was noon, and His Highness still threw out a suggestion for my stay till the evening, if only to present Bherasat Ali Khan. This gentleman is a descendant of the famous Raja Kamgar Khan, who, with a goodly attendance, is travelling in the guise of a small trader, and has strayed so far East in hopes of some assistance from the well-known liberality of the Maharaja. Understanding the rank of the stranger, I have maintained him in befitting comfort, and I wished to see him off with honor before my departure. Every time, however, that I proposed to dismiss the poor but none the less proud nobleman, now specially as I was going away and there was nobody to attend to such customers, His Highness said he would most certainly see him, saying it would be a shame to let a respectable person depart without an interview. I was anxious to dismiss suitably all the strangers, professional and others, before I left, but had succeeded only with respect to Enayet Hossein, (of the Nizamut Court of Moorshedabad,) 'the Prince of Wales's *Sarodi*.' Although I was paying a week's demurrage for my *budgrow*, and the goddess *Doorga* had already arrived within hailing distance, nevertheless, I made up my mind to stay another eight hours for the satisfaction of serving a stranger of a noble stock, in unmerited difficulties.

I could not leave Old Agartala (where the Maharaja now usually resides) before late in the evening. My boat, thrown from pillar to post among the shallows and sands, had a most difficult passage of it in the dark. Towards midnight I reached my house at New Town, where I had supper at 4 in the morning following, the 23rd September (8th Aswin). After breakfast, or an apology for it, cooked, like the supper, in my dining-room, I left New Town—capital of the Tipperah *Raj*—at about 1 O'clock in the day, not before complying with Gopal Sastri's solicitation for a character—that being another of our distinguished visitors. The Howrah had overflowed its banks a day or two before, and though the hill stream in its usual way had been a good deal drained, it was still full enough when we dropped down. We quickly passed the boundary of the *Raj*, into British territory, and reached the first place of any importance, Magra, the head-quarters of the Maharaja's estate of Noornagore, before the shades of evening. We were delayed here some hours in search of auxiliary boats for my cooking and other purposes. For, unluckily for myself, my reserved smaller craft had, at the capital, unknown to me, been impressed into the service of the royal family. The head-man—

the Tehsildar—was not at his post, though not off duty, being on tour through his pergunnah collecting rents, according to the original plan of poor Nilmani Dewan, my predecessor.

But even if the Tehsildar had been at the Magra office, he could hardly have helped us as quickly as could be wished; there are fewer boats than formerly in the boatmen's settlements, while there is a greater demand now-a-days from the Sirkar than before. Since the rise of the jute industry the rayyets now pay more exclusive attention to agriculture. The irregularity in paying for boats at the *Rajbari* is also whispered, but that could scarcely have sufficed in the absence of deeper economic causes to create the diversion. There are hardly any boatmen, pure and simple, in this part of the country, where boats are in request chiefly during the rains when the streams and rivulets and rills are filled, and the veriest stagnant pools and even dry channels are navigable. Then all the boats stowed away in back yards, or sunk in ponds or other waters, are brought out. In former times, when there was little traffic, there was little demand beyond that for the Maharaja's service, the boats being principally used by the people for themselves for going from place to place, even house to house, for going to market or marsh, for going to half-submerged fields to cut grass for their cattle, and so on. In those days, they desired nothing better than engagements for their craft and for themselves as sailors at the *Rajbari*. They were glad thus to eke out their means by this addition to the slender profits of cultivation till, at least, the drier cold weather, when their services might be wanted for cutting and harvesting their own crops. Specie being scarce, this was often their only provision for paying rent. As the Maharaja's tenants, they preferred their hire to be credited to their rent account. If they failed to procure this employment, they failed to pay their rent, and they prayed that it might be in arrear till the next opportunity, and this was usually done. It is all different now. Now-a-days they find it more profitable to attend to their own fields and their own cattle and their own marketing. They are more flush of cash; they not only pay down their rents in money, but often do not know what to do with the balance in hand. They want the services of their own boats, while the demand on all sides, from the development of internal commerce and of inter-local intercourse, is greater than ever, and the supply inadequate. The Maharaja's Noornagore revenue office at Magra, which procures the boats, finds it difficult to supply them, although the *Rajbari* rates are much higher than the prevailing rates; and I suspect the office makes a profit on the transactions. The requisitions have trebled and quadrupled in number, while from improved ideas of comfort and the influx of strangers from far-off places, a superior class of boats of deeper draught is now wanted. I suppose the *Rajbari* must in the not distant future make special arrangements for itself.

I had, some days before my start, sent orders

for two or three boats, but other orders too had arrived for more boats. Small *dingis* might be had but these could not venture out into the Megna. People had, accordingly, gone to fetch larger craft from Brahmanbaria, but had returned unsuccessful. The Tehsildar's assistants went out by water in search to the neighbouring hamlets, but they too came back disappointed. Then they proposed to send to the Tehsildar in the interior. My Afghan orderly accompanied them on the trip, while we slowly led our bark through marshes and channels and submerged fields. The whole country is under water. The bazaar at Magra, the *Pheelkhana*, (elephants' stables,) the temples on the bank of the Howrah, and the Maharaja's office itself, have all become so many islands. I could hardly recognise the land-route by which I had travelled in my palkee from the Teetas up to the capital, through Magra. It is now all under water, more or less. Instead, indeed, of taking the way of the Teetas to the Megna, we took a shorter cut across country. Late in the evening, we anchored near the mouth of a water-course which discharges itself into an extensive marsh, now turned into a small lake. I was for proceeding in order to gain time, but the boatmen would not venture into the lake at night for fear of pirates. We became anxious for the return of my Afghan. I was afraid he might lose his way in this watery waste in the dark, and our journey in consequence be delayed in waiting for him the following day, if he should return even then. At 3 O'clock, however, Mowaz Khan joined the fleet, an hour after we had taken our supper. My monkeys—for I had a small menagerie on board—had not much of an appetite under the strange influence of this journey. It took long to coax them to receive some little sustenance, even a little drink of water. It was a harder task to beguile them into the prison of a cage I had got made for them, but by hook or by crook I succeeded at last, though in the attempt I narrowly escaped biting from the powerful jaws of the larger of my Simian companions, Modu. After I had betaken myself to bed, however, and got within my mosquito curtain, Sir Modu kept up such a doleful cry that I could not help being moved by the gallant knight's appeal. Getting up and out I released both him and his diminutive fellow, and tied them apart, Modu in my own bedroom, notwithstanding, that his rope was stinking disagreeably. Our arms being piled together in a corner, I got them out, and distributed them, to be kept at hand and ready for the reception of unwelcome visitors. My own dagger I specially put under my pillow.

24th September—9th Aswin—Saturday.—As usual, I was the first of my party to get up, although, before going to bed, I had left word with the servants to wake the crew up to weigh anchor and proceed as soon and as fast as possible. I had hardly any rest, and when I opened my eyes, I saw it was already clear dawn, if not day yet. Immediately I ordered the boatmen up, and to work in getting away. It was sometime before we could leave. These fellows want a good deal of 'egging on.' In a little time we came to an embankment bisected by the rivulet we were in. I guessed it was, if not the Brahmanbaria-road, some trunk road in these parts. It is hardly broad enough for a good carriage way, but carriages can, I suppose, pass it during the dry season. At the back of the embankments on the bank of the stream to our left, are a couple of sheds like the lime-house in New Town, lately occupied by the Delhi *hakeem*, looking indeed like (in Indian Pigeon English) a "godown" in the neighbourhood of Calcutta. It turned out to be a cow-house, forming by itself an island, though I saw no cow or bovine conservancy indications in the shape of dung, &c. On the same bank, along the channel, there is here a low, narrow fringe of high ground, a foot above water, on which were a few jungly trees and plants. Further down, on the same side of us, on the extension of this fringe, appeared small bamboo clumps, an occasional giant fig called religious, but no mangoes or jack, with here and there a shed or two—at long intervals a small hamlet. Throughout the tract, however, there were numerous piles of the white dried stalks of the jute piled somewhat after the piling of military arms. We had a glimpse of a couple of temples. We entered Káitalá, unpromising at first sight, but with a good many sheds of habitations scattered about, peeping, rather disconsolately to my mind, through the dark foliage of trees, with water to their very doors. The bank of the channel is lined with trees, mostly jungly and fit for fuel only, and shrubbery, chiefly ratans. We had a sight of the white-limed and green-painted lofty tower of the Roys. It is not on the brook exactly, but a short way from it, from which a short canal leads up to their gate. I believe this piece of water is of their own digging for their own convenience. I was afraid to touch here, or even to show myself at all, for fear of being caught by the Roys, and made a "lion" of, so we hurried past. We met a middle-sized *kose* boat under repairs, evidently belonging to these Squires. Soon we came to a bazaar, with its necessary complement, the "social evil." I felt like the traveller in a strange land, when first he discovered a gibbet—to be in the presence of civilisation. But here, in the centre of this rural solitude, the civilisation seemed to be more that of Timbuctoo, than of any Aryan country, however degenerate. More and more traces of civilisation! This time the representative of the Order might pass muster in Calcutta almost, certainly at Dacca.—Since leaving Agartala, up to this, we have seen hardly any mangoes or jack.

Then we came to the field, whence we had a view of the Káitalá pagoda, which we did not lose sight of for a long time; but we never again had a glimpse of the Squires' towered gate for the vegetation around it. Their house itself we could never discern, not even the famed dancing saloon. After a pretty long course through the open country, we enter villages, passing through the lanes and by-lanes of the dry months, and between the houses of the agriculturists, mostly substantial Mussulmans, our boat actually forcing its way through groves of trees and shrubs, and the powerful network of thickset creepers. Our pets and ourselves, if we chanced to take our positions at the sides, are being choked up with reeds and creepers. I have easily gathered many specimens of the botany of the country, ratans, *pati* (mat) reeds, &c. Modu has frequently been compelled to jump from his post on the window to the water to save himself from the lash of the resisting ratans, and the knockdown blows of other members of the vegetable world. But hark! Loud cries and sobs of women as for the dead assail us. Soon a small covered boat sails past us, conveying weeper or weepers, for we only hear, but do not see, the occupants inside the screens. A family has, doubtless, lost a near and dear one. Perhaps not. A thought strikes me. I look about to enquire. It is hardly necessary. For presently we come upon the band of parted weepers still lingering on the banks of the water, after seeing the covered wherry off. Though the elders are still bellowing, the smaller boys and girls are attracted by our monkeys and audibly discuss them, while their seniors themselves can hardly refrain from casting a glance of curiosity at the animals, if not also their keeper. It is plain that their grief, though real enough, is not quite overpowering. It need not be. For their calamity is only the hopeful sorrow of parting from their daughter *en route* to the home of her husband.

I ask a Mussulman bathing in a neighbouring village the name of the place. It is called Janga or Jangal, and belongs, as he said, to "Gunny Meah Saheb." So the poor tuft-hunter is still no more than the same Gunny Meah of old, even on his own estate, among his own helpless tenantry—his co-religionists. Saheb is, of course, the due of every gentleman. We "poled" on, passing through the estates of Gunny Meah and other Dacca notabilities, like the Mirzas and the Baboos, until, some time after dark, we moored at a village belonging to Hosseini Daroga-e-Ambakhana (so the boatswain said). The whole is a splendid jute country. The holms and banks of creeks and water-courses of British Tipperah are just the kind of soil for the plant. We stop for the night here, as the sailors are reluctant to go ahead, for fear of losing their way in the midst of the great ait of the Megna at the mouth of this tributary stream.

25th September, Sunday.—Left our night's shelter at dawn, and entered the great river. The Megna was, however, in its calmest mood, and we crossed over in no time, comparatively speaking. We then entered the narrow Menakhali, at Baidya Bazaar. The next place close by, is Magrapara Bazaar, Sonargaon—the same where I had once before landed for the purpose of visiting the ruins of ancient Sonargaon

In the bazaar is a school, whose roomy bungalow is the most prominent building—if building, a shed may be called—in the whole place. Near the bazaar to the West is a flight of stairs built by some Ghose (milk-man) where we spent some pleasant hours on our first return from Agartala. The river is now full to the brim ; *then* the water was far, far down, yet sufficient, and disclosing no mud. A good many men are bathing, and women, too ; one of the latter fairish, being olive-complexioned, with the soft delicate features, and fine long hair and clear languishing eyes peculiar to Indian women. She has or has not passed her teens perhaps ; her bust's swelling contour disclosed—without self-consciousness—by the thin single robe (*saree*,) now fitting closer still for the dripping liquid. She is all the better for her poverty, her natural charms undetracted by any monstrosities of gold or silver, miscalled ornaments. Unhappily, however, as though the rose could not be without its thorns, a dirty cotton or linen thread band *(taga)* disfigures her left arm, and perhaps her right also, which is hid under the folds of her robe. Not far from the ghat is a distinguished tree—an old tamarind on a high bank. Parallel to the river runs the public road on the strand, with the telegraph wire alongside. Both road and wire go as far as the junction of this stream with the Megna at Baidya Bazaar, where is a small corrugated iron shed belonging to the Telegraph Department, looking like the booking-office of an inferior railway or steamer station. As there is no railway yet, imagining it to be a signalling office, I at first thought of dropping some message there, but found the door closed. It is an office *in posse*, not yet *in esse*; perhaps only a telegraphic store room for convenience of repairs. A little higher up we come upon a bridge of planks on timber beams, like another in the same road at Baidya Bazaar. Another bridge, and soon another! The fact is this is the military Trunk Road through the heart of Bengal which, passing by way of British Tipperah and Noakhali, goes to Chittagong and the farthest limits of the country on that side. In consequence of its great civil and political importance, no expense is spared on it, and it is kept in very good repair.

Who says there is no beauty in the low plains of Bengal? There is a great deal of poetry, physical and moral, in our fair land, if one has the eye to see and the imagination to give the prospect meaning. Whatever may be the case with the drier yet non-hilly parts, there is much wealth of color and form in the region through which I am travelling. The tropical luxuriance of vegetation, the contrast of land and water, the undulations of waving rice and jute fields fringing the water, which continually crop up between the liquid expanses, and, around the whole, trees of every kind and height, together form a delicious picture; while the humble huts of the poor, peeping through the green foliage, with the children playing to the very edge of the water, and the women laving their slender delicate persons in the crystal stream, now risen up to their very doors, lend a most desirable element of humanity to the scene. The monotony of the everlasting element on which we have been living these days, is, again, finely broken by the constant drift of reed, as well as by green water plants (chief among them the larger *pana*, which is such an enemy to our ponds at home, though doubtless welcome to fish); while the moving huts of small craft and the sailing *bungalows*—as the pinnaces and *budgerows* of superior voyagers may be called—continually passing and repassing, complete the elements of a rich, lively dissolving view.

We have now emerged from the Menakhali or the Sonargaon streamlet into the feeble old channel of the Brahmaputra, now a dry bed for the most part, except during the rains. We stop on the Western bank for a bath and holy purification. My Cashmere pundit and up-country sepoys are already down in the stream.

My gentleman companion now takes his plunge, though without any hopes of the next world. Myself and my sinful valet, Lakir, are still hesitating on this pretence or that. But there is no help for it, we must follow suit or lose our Hindoo credit. While writing, I hear the splash of my Afghan jumping into the sacred waters of the Son of Brahma (Brahmaputra,) while my Brahman cook congratulates him on his turning Hindoo in good company.

It strikes me now that the Sen Rajas must have lived at Rampal in the Dacca country, though history would assign them either Gour or Nuddea for their capital. There is a tradition that Bullal Sen was the son of the river Brahmaputra in the guise of a Brahman. The metamorphosis is unworthy of consideration, but the admission must be accepted. I am inclined to suspect the truth to be that the Royal Reformer, who instituted the order of nobility still known as Koolinism, was a bastard son of a Brahman who had sent his mother the Rani back from the holy watering-place with a full womb, the myth veiling the fact within a religious crust, and changing the disgrace of the reigning family from taint of illegitimacy to the triumph of a Brahmanic connection, and investing Kshattriya royalty with a still more sacred character. It is possible—and that is the most liberal meaning that may be put on the matter—that Ballal's father had for long years prayed in vain for an heir, when, at the suggestion perhaps of some Brahman hermit, he undertook the pilgrimage of the Brahmaputra, and that, whether from the influence of change of scene or from the effect of travelling on the sedentary, his wife conceived there and then, or soon enough thereafter. In this view they may have lived at Gour, or at Nuddea, and only gone on a distant pilgrimage. If they lived in the near Bikrampore, they must have periodically gone to wash their sins in the Brahmaputra, at the same Nangulbund—the holiest spot of the holy river—where a fair is held to this day.

Suvarnagram (popularly Sonargaon) was on the old Brahmaputra, between it and the slender original of the Megna (which, in its present proportions, is a modern stream,) and the Menakhali—a fine situation confined by three waters, and in the neighbourhood of streams like the Lakhya, the Dhaleswari, the Ichhamati, the Booregunga, and the Pudma. No wonder, that the ancient Hindus chose it for a capital, which the Mussulmans after them maintained.

After a dip in the Brahmaputra and breakfast on its breast, we proceed. Instead of descending the sacred stream into the Dhaleswari direct, we enter a water-course running from it to the West, and leading through fields and marshes and ditches and villages to the Lakhya before Naraingunje. We now meet with plantations of the betel leaf, along the bank down to the edge of the water, within a foot to a foot and-a-half. These groves are by no means so completely shaded as the nurseries in our suburban villages of Bonhoogly and Belghoria ;

we could clearly see the contents within. I should note that there are betel sheds also on the banks of the Megna, specially the Western bank, where also we saw the first palms, chiefly areca-nut, coming from the East. The villages on both banks of the water-course we are now 'poling' through are studded with this areca-nut. The cocoanut is not yet seen, nor the fan palm. The date—even that seedy country date which springs unbidden and neglected in every waste on the Eastern boundary of British Tipperah and in Agartala, as in the neighbourhood of Calcutta—is here of a curiosity; the cocoanut is seen only as an article of commerce in the boats. Every house has its mangoes, however, though tamarinds are few and far between, raising their majestic heads of copious hair above the surrounding vegetation. Not a leaf of the jack, so common in Tipperah, has been seen. For the rest, the botany is identical with what we have left in the country higher up: the same bamboos with their slender lithe elastic shafts slowly tapering to the thinest bend or curl and their dense dark yet breathing grove, adorn the prospect on both sides of the Megna ; the same broad-leafed plantain (but not much of it); the same occasional giant cotton ; the same fine-looking forest trees and shrubs of various kinds ; the same thistle-tree called *mon* ; the same *poli* reed ; the same figs, great and small ; the same beautiful ratan.

We are now at Bundur, the seat of a family with a taste for building. I spy through the trees a one-storied brick house, and a fine Indo-Gothic spire of a temple ; they and others all belong to Chandra Mohan Roy and Hari Mohan Roy, the latter of whom had formerly been employed on the Tipperah Maharaja's British estate. I have not yet got a glimpse of their two-storied house. It is here that Jagut Chandra Das has come to live with these village lairds, as one of their medical men. He professes homœopathy ; and doubtless does less execution and less constitutional havoc than the more heroic "medicine men" of other schools and no school. He declares the place to be very unhealthy; quite malarious, and infested by wild beasts. I have just got a view of the two-storied house. The place is on the borders, or perhaps in the midst, of a marsh which, though now full, dries up and festers when the rains are over. The habitable upland is one mass of forest and underwood and is the sporting ground of the Europeans of Naraingunje and Dacca. Naraingunje is hard by, a new and prosperous town which has become a great port, with European connections, within the last twenty years. As soon as we left the Brahmaputra channel and entered the back country, we spied the smoke of the Naraingunje factories, and even the masts of the shipping, and now we are close upon the port. Bundur, though now such a jungle, seems from its name to have been an ancient port before the rise of Naraingunje.

At Naraingunje at last, a good margin of day remaining!

It is something to have done with these boatmen, and their Chief.

This commander, Ram Charan, the son of Harihar the Great (so distinguished according to a dutiful and not overmodest son), is a vain old bore of the first water, quite capable of any impertinence. A pariah by caste, he has all the insolence of the prosperous vulgar which led my great progenitor Manu, the lawgiver, to denounce and repress the wealth of the servile Order. The water-men would not mind you, supported doubtless by their substantial chief. It required great and unceasing efforts to move them or bring them from old Agartala within a reasonable time, or to make them do any honest mortal thing. Rebuke? Why, they anticipated you by having the first word! After that, of course, all your eloquence falls flat on the knowing rascals. By pure neglect and cruelty of the worst kind, they not only lost the best of our hill parrots, but caused the poor thing to perish in the most pitiable plight. Drowned in durance vile—cooped in his cage—was that eloquent *myna*, whom I had not had the heart to part with to cousin Doyal's son Jangi Bahadoor (as I love to call my Babooling), notwithstanding all his entreaties. These wretches had dropped the cage, without moving a finger to pick it up from the water or even allowing us an opportunity for rescue. What unavailing struggles did the parrot pass through before death closed the scene! I was truly sorry for the *myna*, and was more than ever confirmed in my opinion against confining animals. If all this sound weak, there is no help for it; it is God's appointment that we should love his creatures that are lovable. We cannot escape from our hearts. For my part, I never invite pets. It is too great a responsibility. As for the pleasure of their company, they cause distress likewise. Besides the accident to the parrot, the domestic animals which, notwithstanding my habitual avoidance of such connections, gathered round me at Agartala, have given me no little trouble and anxiety. The antelope, the monkeys, and the parrots, accompany me. The pariah dogs and cats that joined my establishment unasked and lived upon me, could not be so transported. At any rate, I could not make the attempt without incurring the suspicion of lunacy. All I could do was to leave some instructions for their feed. The parting was a trial to both sides. The pantomime, which was more than usually mute, was inexpressively melancholy. It was plain they felt that their patron and provider was leaving them, perhaps for ever. I say "perhaps" doubtfully, for on a previous occasion Tom the pariah dog behaved in my absence as if he expected my return—unless the poor fellow abandoned himself to my memory in the spirit of the Hindu widow mourning for her lord. When I was there, he would often be absent on his wars with the surrounding powers, great and small, of the lower animal world, his expeditions against the jackal tribe, and so on. In my absence, he stuck to the house like a nail and defended it, when need was, like a hero. Tom was no Cerberus to be silenced with a sop. He was absolutely above temptation. He starved himself at his post of self-elected duty, resisting even the invitations of my neighbours to come and eat at theirs, and only thankfully accepting anything that the human guard (who took their meals elsewhere) in pity brought him. His fidelity was put to a formidable test. The British Commissioner and the British Magistrate came together on a visit. The Political officer in charge at the Agency was with his family occupying the Agency bungalow, so the Commissioner, whose family were with him, put up at the Maharaja's guest-house, and the Magistrate pitched his camp in my garden. Tom, after the first salutation with a bark from the verandah, held his tongue, looking sullenly perhaps, but, beyond watching the proceedings of the mighty intruder, forbearing to interfere. After a day or two the weather became severe or from some other inconvenience, the stranger wanted to remove to the bungalow, or a part thereof. Then came the tug of war. Tom resisted what he regarded as British encroachment with a courage which the bravest of native Princes might envy. Not till "that villainous saltpetre" was brought into play, could he be dislodged. But if before the vile gun, he retreated, he did not give up the fight, but behaved himself as a soldier still. It was a sight to the people of the little Principality to see the representative of British power pursuing the poor pariah about in the neighbourhood, through by-path and road, in plain and under cover. Tom eluded the enemy and his infernal engine. But no sooner the instrument was down than Tom was again to the fore. Tom, however, was too loyal a subject of the Imperial crown to show his teeth. Like his human countrymen, he employed only constitutional opposition. Agitation was his utmost weapon for the maintenance of his rights. It is hopeful to know that it succeeded. Nature has denied his kind quill, but Tom was blessed with the gift of the gab, and he used it to better purpose than my friend Surendra Nath Banerjee ever did, until the good Englishman was glad to return to his tent, leaving Tom master of the field—and the house.

These pets and outcasts have given me a severe pang at parting. Poor Tom, the noble pariah dog, is, I wish to heaven I could say, gone. Alas! he was only going, too slowly perhaps for him but surely. He was suffering dreadfully from fatal sores all over, specially in the head. He bore it up like a hero that he was. By pure power of will, he kept himself from running mad. The best of us would be furious, under less than his complaint! I may here say that I have seen better brutes than men. The dogs are indeed the noblest creatures of God. The three noblest beings within my knowledge were three perfect canine gentlemen —one a Newfoundland, another of some large

European breed, and the third a Bengali pariah, my poor Tom.

At Naraingunje I took steamer the following day, and went by the familiar track to Goalundo, and so on to Calcutta.

JOURNEY TO

INDEPENDENT TIPPERAH

IN 1884.

CALCUTTA TO DACCA.

IN going to Dacca I wished to avoid, if possible, the crowd and bustle of the daily despatch from Goalundo. I set my heart upon the good *Princess Alice*, Captain Atkinson, in which large steamer I had many a time voyaged, and with whose commander and his family I was well acquainted. Accordingly, I made previous enquiries at the Sealdah Office as to the timing of that vessel. I learnt that she left Goalundo on Friday mornings. I must, therefore, start by the Thursday evening train to catch her.

But Thursday was out of the question for the good Hindu. The old Rishis had set their faces against it and the dutiful son of Bharadwaj could not think of it, on pain of the combined hostility of all the heavenly powers. Not even to win a kingdom—so the law runs—should anybody venture out on a Thursday evening. But as modern lawyers can laugh at the most elaborate precautions of the legislators of the day, so there are ways, thoroughly orthodox, of cheating the Rishis and gods. The preceding day was a most auspicious one, and I took advantage of it to make my ceremonial exit, making the stars believe I left on Wednesday. The affair was simple enough, though not without its inconveniences. Within the specified hour of that Wednesday—for the whole day was not blessed—I abandoned one apartment of my residence, (not before passing through the prescribed forms) not to enter it again till my return from the contemplated journey, and was supposed to be on my travels.

The start *de facto*—the material start—took place the next day. It is my wont to keep my movements as far to myself as practicable. Regard being had to the weakness and disadvantages of our race—to our own inordinately developed bump of "eye-shame," as we call it, to our institutions, our social and domestic system which gives so many strangers-in-fact a claim upon our deference or kindness, our reluctance to refuse,—considering all these, that is the only possible policy. If one would not either risk a miscarriage of his arrangements or incur the reproach of rudeness, he had better go and come as quietly as possible, and even suddenly as it were. This time the same course was more particularly recommended to me by circumstances. Only a few friends, therefore, were apprised of my intentions, and they were enjoined secrecy. I was thus at liberty to attend to my business and make my preparations, without attracting notice and without interruption. So, accompanied by a few friends, I drove to the station. I had followed the old injunction to take time by the fore-lock, beyond the letter—with a vengeance—for I anticipated the ancient gentleman. Under pressure of over-careful or nervous advisers, I was preposterously early. My traps and my servants—a goodly lot—had preceded me. The mail train by which I was to travel was not yet alongside. Another train was expected, and not before it came and discharged its passengers and was removed to a corner, would my up-train enter appearance. I passed the time walking up and down the long platform or admiring the "Mammoth Pavilion" of the terminus—the long, broad and deep saloon or hall which serves for waiting-room of the third class millions. While thus strolling I saw a European, who sat on a bench in the platform, salaam to me. I involuntarily stopped a moment and then passed on, without returning the compliment. He repeated the motion. I became uneasy, looked at the friend who was walking next me, on the chance of the welcome being offered to *him*, and then turned my head round, to see if the greeting was given to a European behind my shoulder. Not seeing any such god about and not knowing what to make out of the matter, and, truth to say, being ashamed to face the White monster of goodwill to a Baboo, I did not turn back, but pursued the walk on. Of course, I was not fool enough to think that a perfect stranger, and, above all, a genuine White, would smile and bow to me in right earnest—nay, that he would repeat the courtesy. For once I was mistaken. It is not a bad world, after all. We are said to feed angels unawares sometimes. Besides, there are angels in office and angels out of it. Even the Ilbert Bill plague has not apparently extinguished the genus. Here at least was an angel unmistakable—or a veritable monster! But not yet! Not before another turn in my walk brought me face to face with the queer Whiteman, was the phenomenon explained to my wondering mind. Meanwhile, I espied a train on a fresh line of rails laid alongside of the old line immediately to the North of the platform under a newly raised but lower shed—looking like a child on the lap of the lofty-housed main station. Having ample time on my hands, we repaired to see the new bantling. Arrived at the minor concern, I met an intelligent Behari Jemadar who has been twenty-one years on the Railways, with whom I started a conversation. He is a good fellow, not at all inclined to be rude like other railway myrmidons. I learnt from him that the traffic on the new Bengal Central Railway was not only good but likely to surpass the most sanguine expectations. Already the passengers are plentiful, and this is but the beginning—the line having just opened. During the last bathing festival the passenger traffic was enormous. The Company could not provide rolling stock enough, to say nothing of passengers' cars. Anything on wheels was welcome. The whole Hindu population of Jessore especially, seemed to be astir and besieged the stations for a lift to the Hooghly branch of the holy Ganges. Men, women and children crowded horse boxes and animal vans and goods trucks, glad to have standing place. It was an awful passenger visitation. The railway agency collapsed under the strain. The booking regulations were suspended. Tickets could not possibly be provided fast enough for so many at a time. The unsympathetic British administration would have maintained the system, to the eternal disappointment of thousands, but that the lust of lucre recommended the cause of the poor pilgrims. So good an opportunity for making money at the outset of the career of a line could not be lost. So the booking Baboos were drawn out of their dark dens inaccessible, to sally forth into the open, where, their number much strengthened, they received the fare from applicants and showed each the way to the train. It was no time to calculate or to count. In the midst of the rush and crush—

before the surging crowd—any sum was demanded and any sum received and pocketed without examination or return of change, or thought as to the extent of accommodation provided. The numbers of the passengers were scarcely ascertained. I hope the Company will soon perfect their arrangements, so as to avoid a recurrence of the scandal. I would suggest to the Traffic Manager a study of the Hindu almanac, to take his measures in accordance with its indications. I did not leave this junior station before making some kind personal inquiries regarding my good informant. He was not without his grievances ; indeed, he sighed in disappointment at the absence of recognition of native fidelity and usefulness. From what I could judge, no Indian Railway need want a better servant of his class. I do not remember his not sonorous name, nor would it be proper to mention it if I did. I hope he may catch the eye of a worthy Superintendent or Manager.

On my return stroll, I encountered the same British welcome that had puzzled me. This time there could be no mistake, and I quickly returned the salute and rounded it off to a fine bend of my turbaned head, to make up for my previous non-recognition and unwitting rudeness. After another walk or so, fairly tired, I took my seat on the bench and drew my gracious "ruler" into conversation. In fact, I could not resist the temptation to learn something about him, and so quietly and cautiously plied him. He was a Private of H. M.'s—Foot, now stationed at Dum Dum. It is a Welsh regiment though he is an Englishman. The Welsh element is not by any means overwhelming, yet the Cambrian dialect is freely spoken in it, the only regiment in the army in which it is allowed. Many of the Welsh do not know English at all. My man is a good specimen of the British Private, devoid neither of intelligence nor of information about his regiment or the army, but without either dignity or enthusiasm, and indifferent to other peoples. With him I had a short not uninstructive conversation, if leading him through a catechism might be so called. My enquiries were for the most part calculated to draw out public information. Some, however, were more personal, though insinuated with kindness and caution. But neither by the one set nor the other, nor in any other way, could I gather the grounds of his strange condescension. He was very far from mad or imbecile, though, in his behaviour in question, he was sufficiently mysterious. I once for a moment cogitated whether the phenomenon might have something to do with my swell Sirdari turban, but I soon dismissed the idea. Though I do not maintain the Light of Allah on my face, and my height is by no means Highland, yet I am frequently enough taken for a chief of the North West Border. But that delusion commands no such deference. I may get through a miscellaneous crowd of Indians and Anglo-Indians on easy terms, but without special greetings, from the latter at all events. For, even an Afghan is but a native, after all. Happily all speculation was set at rest before I left Sealdah. Tom Atkins was no monster; he was too human, perhaps. In the most delicate way, he threw out a hint that he was filled with anxiety about thoughts of the morrow. I eagerly lent ear to so prudent a defender of my native land. The army could scarcely be in arrears of payment, but vague visions of the poor soldier's difficulty in meeting the wants of a numerous family flitted across my mind and enlisted on his behalf all my Oriental sympathies. But no such thing! My Tom cat had anticipated Mr. Punch's famous counsel. He was, in fact, a Benedick, without his Beatrice. By and bye the truth was disclosed. He had been out holiday-making in town and had spent his last farthing. He did not expect to see coin before next pay-day. And the thought that oppressed him was, how to provide for his next morning's—beer! I wanted no more. It was enough revelation. I could appreciate the good fellow's wise resolve to avoid debt, and I thoroughly understood his reluctance to ask a comrade or even a countryman. For the rest, I confess myself sinner enough to sympathise with a poor uneducated man of ample leisure, in his slavery to a pernicious habit.

My adventure with the Railway officials was of a more prosaic kind, and absolutely provoking. In paying my reckoning for myself and party and things, I had a hot Currency Question with them—a question which had no solution for me, but remained stiff and frowning. Their demand by the first calculation amounted to Rs. 90 odd and I offered a note for Rs. 100. It was a new crisp fresh British Indian "greenback," lately issued by the Currency Office and received only the day before from another Government department. Imagine, then, my amazement when I discovered that, of all places in the world, at the Calcutta terminus of the Eastern Bengal Railway, now a State concern, it was not legal tender! The idea of returning me change was, of course, out of the question. They'd none of it, change or no change. In vain my people explained and entreated the clerks. The Government scrip was no currency on the Government railway. In vain my friends appealed to the Lord of the Terminus. My friends might be ever so respectable—and they included barristers, Presidency Magistrates and editors—but, for any assistance that I got from them in that dilemma, they proved the veriest scum of earth. The Railway King was inexorable ; I must bring silver and that of the Calcutta mint. British dross —the sterling majesty of sovereigns—would have been spurned by His Imperial Majesty of Sealdah. It was a pretty predicament for a traveller to be in, with a whole lot of camp-followers and baggage of rather expeditionary proportions. There was not much time left, it having been nearly all consumed in argument and expostulation and entreaty at different business centres at the station. Certainly there was no more time to go home for coined bullion and little prospect, at that evening hour, of changing the note at the neighbouring money-scriveners'. I had no other alternative to betake to than a leisurely retreat. I summoned up all my philosophy to reconcile me to my hard lot. It was plain that I could not go on my journey that day, notwithstanding all my previous care to propitiate the gods and stars, and there was nothing for it but to submit to the loss and disappointment with a good grace. That is easier said than done. My submission in especial was a tragic business, entailing, from dislocation of arrangements, severe inconveniences to one and all of my party, and involving the gravest consequences to myself. Practically it meant the loss of a week. If I missed that evening's chance I must wait another seven days to be able to avail myself of the convenience of the larger steamer from Goalundo. It seemed plain that the stars were not going to be cheated. After all, the evil principle of the day and hour—Thursday evening—must triumph, and I was to be made an example of and be heavily punished for my disregard of scripture and defiance of the heavenly orbs presiding over human destiny, in-dependance perhaps on the dicta of an ancient blue-stocking, a philosopher in *saree*—Khona—at any rate for what might be deemed trifling with the law and adopting a policy of finesse and sharp practice towards the gods and planets. In this moment of despair my good genius turned up on the scene in the shape of a friendly official—a Justice of the Peace and a Magistrate—no Honorary figure-head, but a regular stipendiary reality—and what not besides. At the advent of the great man there was a sudden change in my affairs. His very name acted as a charm on the rude railway establishment—his presence was a power of beneficence. Before he was fairly in the station—as soon as he was in sight and my masters understood from my men that he was coming to see me off,—my fortunes revived. Suddenly there came a relaxation in the hard and fast rule of the little men dressed in brief authority. The martinet was in a moment metamorphosed into the courtier. The whole machinery seemed in a moment to be oiled with the grease of conciliation and sympathy. There was a corresponding change on the Bourse. The Public Credit, collapsed the previous second, at once revived. Government scrip again found buyers. There was even a demand. My note was recalled after having been peremptorily rejected. The Paper Currency that had before been at such discount, again fetched sixteen annas to the rupee. They not only accepted my note as legal tender but, when it was found that the railway demand upon me was full one hundred rupees, they seemed sorry for the loss of opportunity to humour me with change in any form I might like!

Thus I left Calcutta by the mail to Goalundo. It was a comfortable uneventful journey. For my adventures and troubles vanished with the start, and did not show disposition to reappear before we reached Goalundo landing. The railway often gives one bad neighbours and strange bed-fellows. I had no inconvenient customers. Between myself and my companion, we occupied the whole saloon or apartment. Sole inmates of our snug little furnished shanty in motion, we were lords of all we surveyed. Sometimes, indeed, a journey happily begun has ended miserably. On more than one occasion, in the course of my railway travelling by night, I remember having opened my eyes on a horrible incubus in the shape of a naked Whiteman, (who had stolen into the room unperceived during my sleep,) suspended in a berth above me! This time I had not invoked the gods in vain. No such surprises were in store for me on this trip. We ended as we began—the only two occupiers of our carriage. We lounged and conversed, alternately, at our sweet will, undisturbed, all the while advancing in our journey, making, indeed, wonderful progress without effort of our own, almost unperceived, thanking the Genius of Modern Science and, above all, acknowledging the goodness of that Providence which, by bringing us under British sway, had given us a full share of the blessings of improvement which we had had no hand in originating. We had had our midday meals late in the afternoon and no other eating before the start;—our minds and hands were too full for any appetite. This railway pull is a good stomachic. In a few short hours we were decidedly hungry. So we produced our commissariat and fell upon it with a quiet energy. Having had our fill and stowed away our stores in their proper places under the seats and removed all traces of war or execution, we filled our pipes and smoked our hookas as we chewed our betels, till we snored away into unconsciousness.

Morning disclosed to us the wide sweep of the everlasting Ganges—great still if not holy

—its ends lost in the mist of the distance—type of the antiquity, the grandeur, the vastness and the mystery of India! But a sense of imminent personal danger arrests poetical reflection. The train seems to be hurried right into the bosom of the yawning stream! But it is a momentary fear. Suddenly Jehu draws in and soon stops, and you find yourself close to the water, abreast of the steam Despatch. A lot of coolies attack our traps. In vain my companion tells them that we have servants to carry twice as much as our luggage. The fellows have to be repulsed by sheer force. They retire not from the field, however, but hover about it, biding their time, like jackals in the rear of Indian battle. They were right—an unerring instinct surely guides them. Thus, the 3rd class not being quickly released, my people could not come to my assistance, and being apprehensive of pressure of time, I acquiesced in the employment of these intrusive porters. Followed by them, I marched to the larger steamer lying at a short distance, understanding her to be the *Princess Alice.* I was thwarted at every step. Every body thought it his duty to oppose me. All pointed the Despatch to me, as if I had suddenly been afflicted with blindness. I protested in vain. In vain I said I was not going by the Despatch. That was the only conveyance they said. Some of my own coolies slunk unperceived to the Despatch. Nor did my own *princely* mistress prove more kind. The crew of the flat (the *Princess*' own maid of honour as well as of all work) lying nearest land, through which one must go on board the steamer, railed at my folly. The European commander of the flat volunteered the agreeable information that in their steamer and under their sailoring, I might reach Naraingunje in fifteen days ! But I was not to be shaken in my resolution, long since made. Another and worse difficulty appeared, however. My booked luggage had been taken into the Despatch. I might require on board some of the things ; besides, some of the trunks contained costly articles which I would not, without particular safeguards, consign to the tender mercies of railway servants, far from my reach. So Babu Kumud Nath, my companion, hastened to the Despatch to procure release of the packages. As there was little time remaining to start, he proposed to go by the Despatch. I, however, got alarmed at the prospect of a Selkirk life on board. Knowing as I did that I would be the only party there, besides commander and crew, I did not at all relish the idea of separation from Kumud Nath. Accordingly, I begged him to return by all means, with or without the luggage. Meanwhile, I made for the *Princess Alice*. On reaching the upper deck, I found I was unaccompanied by my followers. On enquiry, I found they had been stopped by the crew. On mentioning it to the commander, he ordered my things up. In explanation he said that nobody travelled by that steamer, in consequence he occupied the whole front of the upper deck with his family. He, however, quickly ordered a couple of rooms to be cleared for me. It was time to start and I grew anxious about my luggage in the Despatch and, above all, apprehensive of leaving Kumud Nath in the lurch. I had also to send some telegrams, but the telegraph office was at Goalundo station proper, which is some miles distant inland. I was looking out for some one whom I could trust to send. There had been a change in the command. My old friend Atkinson was no longer Captain. But his successor did not seem forbidding, so I made bold to mention my difficulty. I was ready to pay for the trouble if he could recommend a confidential man who would be sure to deliver my messages instead of throwing them into the river and pocketing the money. The Captain kindly undertook to send my messages for me. I was, then, in want of ink, though paper and pen I possessed. He brought me an ink-pot and produced his own telegraph book for me to write my messages in, which he sent off. This was a great relief, and I heartily blessed the good commander. Meanwhile, Kumud Nath was in a precarious state —as traveller only, of course, God be praised! He had left the Despatch boat at the moment before its start and was hurrying forward along the beach to catch my *Princess* at the time that we were about leaving. His fate hung in the balance. A few seconds—a moment—remained to decide it. A sudden fit of cough or sneezing might have left him wondering or crying in vain on that desolate shore, in that purgatory of a railway terminus, without accommodation, divorced from his traps, without perhaps any money in his pocket. I was in almost as great an anxiety on his account as he was himself on his own. At that moment I greatly missed the good Captain, whom I would have appealed to, if I could find him. However, the distress was of short duration. After all, Kumud Nath jumped into the temporary draw-bridge connecting the flat with the land at the point of its withdrawal, and ran up breathless to the steamer through the *Princess Alice's* flat. He had failed to get the luggage removed. The trunks were booked for Dacca and the Company would not allow of their transfer on the way.

I was much disappointed in not finding old Atkinson in command, for to see him was not the least of the motives which actuated me in electing the tedious passage by the larger steamer, in preference to the quick journey by the Despatch. The present commander was too good to speak ill of his predecessor, but I was not long on board without learning that there had been many changes among the railway staff and much complaining and counter-complaining and quarrelling and intrigue and, perhaps, some injustice. I had no reason to be dissatisfied with the present Captain, in fact, I have already acknowledged his courtesy. He is a rather heavy unprepossessing man but sound withal; accomplished in his profession, of wide experience on sea and river, sober and steady, attentive to work, with a good temper, kind and accessible to his men. We had not many opportunities of conversing, for he was all day busy, and out of work he was a man of family; but I found him a man of intelligence and was interested in his experiences in the China and Arabian seas. He had brought down the Maharaja of Tipperah in 1882 from Nabinagar, at the junction of the Teetas with the Megna, to Goalundo. The Maharaja was so satisfied with him that on his return from his pilgrimmage to Brindaban, he expressed a desire to be carried back by the same Captain and had him and his steamer brought down for him at Goalundo. It is not a little creditable to the Captain that, having had to do with a native prince and his attendants in two voyages, he breathed not a syllable against any one of them. Almost any other Anglo-Indian would have been sure to retail a dozen stories, many of them grossly exaggerated if not actually manufactured, against the Raja and his family and servants, and generally to speak flippantly and contemptuously of them. I have seen English gentlemen abuse the hospitality of native gentlemen and princes by speaking ill of them.

I always enjoy the river view of Dacca. After the absence of several years, it was interesting to me to come to the old city. The scene was the same that I had left, rather better perhaps, for one or two improvements. The most noticeable change was the completion of the fine mansion of Raghu Baboo, the well-known banker. He and his brother have been spending a good deal of money, in marriages and entertainments to Europeans in consequence. I trust the habit will stick, and not be confined to occasions matrimonial, on which the most faint-hearted of the caste is wont to be liberal and profuse. It is a good thing to spend—for those who *have*, and the Dasses have more than they can hoard.

IN THE HEART OF BENGAL PROPER.

July 24th, 1884, Thursday.—Left early in the morning our night's mooring at the mouth of the creek at the Baktávali Sands. Entering the narrow channel, we poled through it, until it mingled with the rice fields at the back of the left bank of the Booree-Gunga and was finally lost in the great bogs and fens. The marshes are all apparently full, but the lower paddy tracts are barely navigable, although the season is far advanced.

At 9 O'clock we sight the back of Narain-gunje, but it was a good hour's pull before we reach the outskirts of the town. The channel widens at this junction into an extensive water. The current here is strong against us, and the boat is thrown back, notwithstanding all hands are at the oars and the poles. By long and earnest effort we succeed in getting out of the creek, but not before the boat is drawn on purpose close to the bank, to the left, where the current is comparatively milder, and patiently, prudently and slowly pulled forward. Pass some picturesque villages at the flank of Naraingunje. The houses of the substantial rayyets, cultivators of jute, are reached from the water through fine natural coverts, the trees and plants and creeping bush having disposed themselves easily into groves over the water. The women and little girls are at work near the water upon the jute-plant, already cut, their both wrists adorned with bracelets of different kinds. Others, young men and women —more specially the latter—stand up to see us, mute and motionless but for the slow turn of the head to follow us, waiting and watching with patient curiosity till we were wholly out of sight. The women are modest enough—without any forwardness indeed, yet without any of the shrinking timidity of dames of other and better classes. The vegetation is for the most part the same as in East Bengal generally, the most valuable of the big trees being mango, areca, and bamboo. These are everywhere throughout the journey. Others, less regarded by the people, attracted my notice. One black knotty tree, apparently wild, with beautiful round leaves, I particularly remarked constantly recurring, and another cultivated little tree with fine large well-ribbed foliage, somewhat like *Amra (Spondias Mangifera)* leaves but larger, or like Champa (*Michelia Champaka*) but of deeper blue-green and more distinctly ribbed. The force of the tide kept us long before a timber-yard serving for a boat-dock. The water has advanced up to the foot of the scaffolding for cutting timber. One large Upcountry boat for conveying heavy goods is lying under repairs. Next is a European factory, brick-building towered by a lofty chimney, with long bamboo sheds hard by on one side and a thatched bungalow for residence of the Whiteman, on the other. Farther on, right in the centre of the vast liquid area formed by the confluence of the creek and the river, rises before us a neat little cottage without any trace of an inmate of any kind. It might be thought deserted but that it was brand new and had the appearance of waiting for its first occupants. It is an architectural puzzle. Consisting as it does of a longish tiled brick-built shed on an elevated foundation of masonry, screened in front by a brick wall near the edge of the yard, approached by two flights of steps leading down to the water,—what could be the object of such a curious structure at such a place? we wondered. It is evidently too rich for the poor and too poor for the rich. Without out-offices or conveniences of any kind, it is obviously unfit for habitation. To us, in truth, it looked like one of the Municipal *tatties* or public privies in Calcutta. We kept up enquiry until the truth was disclosed—it was the new Burning Ghat for the disposal of the Hindu dead. Having hazarded so many guesses and we confessing our defeat, we feel bound to acknowledge that it is a prince of a Hindu cemetery or rather cremation-ground—for situation. Although opposite to two European factories—namely—the one just mentioned and another next to it now undergoing repairs (after having been apparently closed for sometime),—it is a good way off from the town proper of Naraingunje. It was a happy idea of the Municipality to shunt the inevitable nuisance away from the habitable world to the middle of the water. Of course, it was a happy idea according to time and place. The antique Lake-dwellers would probably have discountenanced it among them. It would make little difference among an urban community of modern Chinese—many of whom habitually reside in family boats—whether a burning business was transferred from land to water or from water to land. When the port of Naraingunje has made more progress within the next few years, and a busier as well as more numerous mercantile community have gathered around the new Burning Ghat, invading its insular solitude, and craft of every kind have crowded the river and rivulet, making the loneliness of the Burning Ghat resound to a thousand cries, what may now be regarded as a suitable situation for the nuisance will be found inconvenient enough. At Calcutta, for instance, it would be a dangerous experiment, besides an intolerable eye-sore and nose-sore, to set up a Cremation Yard in the bosom of the river, in the centre of the port. Indeed, the Naraingunje solution of the Burning Ghat problem would be impossible in the Hooghly river generally, even if such islets (*churs*) as at Narainjunge were obtainable there. In our part of the country, on both banks, the cremation grounds have existed in their places from time immemorial. The Hindu communities having long since acquired a vested right to burn their dead in the particular sites, any attempt to disturb them would cause the greatest outcry. Men like Ram Gopal Ghose, who do not believe in the sanctity of either the river or the burning operation, would start up to defend the privilege of their orthodox, however misguided, countrymen. An illustration of the strength of the sentiment in such matters and of the readiness of demagogues to utilise it to their purposes, was recently offered by the agitation in respect of the slaughter-house at Barrackpore. A Bengalee contemporary, week after week, thundered against the outrage of locating the shambles in the immediate vicinity of a Hindu temple there. Other papers followed suit, the vernacular press in especial making the grievance its own. If I remember aright, only one paper, supposed to be partial to paradox, and certainly independent of party, kept its own counsel. With more caution than its fellows, it moved not, ignoring the subject altogether. It showed at once wisdom and strength. No little firmness was required to resist the current. Nor, apparently, could there have been any risk in adopting a reiterated report from a brother-editor known to reside in the immediate neighbourhood of the alleged occurrence. For all that, the one journalist saved his credit by not allowing himself to be deceived by appearances. A friend of mine, who soon after visited Barrackpore, took the opportunity to inquire. It was with difficulty he could discover a little image of Kali in a small lower-room. There was no other building which could, by any courtesy, be called a temple. By "temple," if it had any meaning or reality, this Kali hole must have been understood by the imagination of the fervid Defender of the Faith. My friend now inquired after the grievances of the priests. The head-man replied almost in the words of the famous Knife-grinder—

Story? God bless you! I have none to tell, Sir.

My friend, with his cue from an intelligent and free press, was not to be thus baulked, any more than the Friend of Humanity with his enthusiasm of Humanity and wild sympathy for the poor. He pressed the point specifically. Which was the new slaughter-house? No answer. The charge was renewed. Was there no place for slaughtering cattle? The poor priests shut their ears against the unholy sound and turned their faces. The conversation was evidently getting outrageous. Still my friend would not retire from the field without his parting shot. So he discharged, without faltering, the query final on the guardians of the goddess—But wasn't there a place for killing animals? The mild Hindu Druids, almost in despair, mustered up politeness to reply—pointing to the spot in front of the goddess—"*There* is our place for *sacrifice* [of lambs]; we know no other place or operation." On his way back, my friend kept attacking right and left all whom he met with, but in vain. Then, by the merest chance, he espied in the distance a new building, apparently a small factory, on the bank of the river, away from any habitation, and enquired what it might be. They did not know. Was it a mill, or other like place of business? They knew not. Still pursuing his search as he went, he at last heard from some one, evidently more knowing than the rest, something to the purpose that arrested him. This deponent believed it to be something like a slaughtering-place—some kind of meat stall or enclosure for butchers' business, as he had been told, said he, but did not know. And so it was; my friend could at last cry—Eureka! That was, indeed, the long-sought slaughter-house. For any external evidences, it might be anything else, from a place of business to a place of prayer. There were no bones about, and of course no prowling vulture nor feathery adjutant with the unerring instinct—a far more useful officer in the economy of human society than his namesake in Her Majesty's Army. So much for the righteous indignation of an independent press!

And here I would put in a word. I would recommend to our countrymen the old injunction, Look before you leap. I would especially entreat my brethren of the quill, Look before you profess to see. Before you dip your pen, *know*. Above all, throw not your vitriol ink about you, without examining and making sure of what you are about. Weigh well your words —think of their effect—and, for God's sake, remember your responsibility. On you depends the existence of the Free Press of India. It will be foolish for Government, for your sins or any others', to abolish the liberty of journalism, but it is just possible—nay, it is not an improbable contingency. In fact, it is said to be on the cards! So take heed betimes. Criticise as sharply as you feel,—for, a press that will not do so is worse than useless and had better not be,—but stick to facts; never invent calumnies, never imagine grievances: you surely can help *that*.

We crossed over to the opposite bank of the Lukha, leaving Naraingunje to the left, not forgetting to store in in the hold the celebrated water of that river from mid-stream. From a distance we were hailed by the bustle and noise of busy Madangunje, evidently in market assembled. Leaving the *Hát* to the right, we entered the inlet opposite Naraingunje. Wide at the junction, the brook for the rest was scarcely wider than our broad boat. We were pulled through thickets of bamboo and other plants and creepers, between the grass-roofed houses of the peasantry. We soon passed the fine village of Bahar, with its brick and stucco manor-houses of the Zemindars and its noble temple, whose steeple peeps at you through the surrounding vegetation from a long distance. I have often, during my passage to and fro, wished to touch here to make the acquaintance of these Baboos buried in such picturesque solitude. But I have as often been too hurried home or to my business farther East to fulfil my wish. The country seems almost wild, but, so far from being desolate, it is a living scene clothed in Nature's choicest woodland drapery and instinct with the romance of still life in the Tropics.

But it is a dark scowling romance—in the midst of that life death lurks, in all its horrid shapes. Certainly, the Baboos' village is over-run with too much rank vegetation for their health. By the afternoon we had crossed unperceived the old Brahmaputra into the Minakhali Khal which passes Sonargang. At the close of the day, we sighted the Megna and moored in the Khal opposite Baidyabazar.

25th July, Friday.—As we approached the Megna last evening, the atmosphere became breezy—a bad omen for our safe and speedy voyage. It blew stronger and stronger, making us uncomfortable in the present and frightening us in regard to our future. We were compelled to close all our shutters for fear of both wind and insects. Late in the night, the breeze somewhat abated; still there was no complete cessation. In the morning, it was faint enough, still the boatmen were not for moving out of our mooring. Their fear was a pretence, we thought; certainly, we were for venturing somehwat, or at least trying, rather than vegetate in this stagnant channel. So we bullied them into letting the boat down the river, broad and deep, before us. So the important voyage began. With scarcely disguised reluctance and visible misgivings, they started on the oblique sailing 'cross stream. The Brahman's Son—the river-god—was not in his best mood. The Pacific Ocean of rivers was far from pacific. The water was in a gentle simmer. We thought we might brave it. We did not discover our danger till too late when we found ourselves far away from land on either side. The element in mid-stream was in a more decided ferment. But there was nothing for us now but to go through it like men. The commander and his men pricked up courage to the sticking point and brought into play their utmost pluck and science. We watched in anxiety and trepidation as the boat was rocked on the undulating liquid, until it was led right into the midst of the rice fields in the bosom of the river. Crossing the rice field, we came upon another less broad part of the river, which we crossed. Behold another rice tract and at its end another river as it were! But there is no end to the succession of land and water and *quasi* land! Passing the last-mentioned channel, we entered another shallow piece of water with the eternal rice plant apparently suspended in it, after which we came upon another minor channel but deep. We entered another paddy field, passing through which we came upon another minor part of the Megna. Not before we crossed this too, or the greater part of it, did we come within safe distance of the left or Tipperah bank of the great river. We had strained our nerves to the utmost in unison with the efforts of our men as they made for yonder village to our right. On entering the rice lands skirting the hamlet, we felt relieved in proportion to our previous tension. "God be praised!" cried I involuntarily, in recognition of our safety. We even congratulated ourselves on a cheap bargain. Having gained the village or its adjoining fields so quickly and without a scratch, we were disposed to make light of the famous "middle passage" and thought the great Megna not quite broad enough. But we had sung "safe!" before we were well out of the wood. Our trial was far from over. The paddy was real Nature's grass, and the houses on the bank along which we were coursing were real human habitations, and the bamboo sticks by which our boat was propelled onwards was no less real, yet for purposes of our absolute safety they might just as well have been all *Maya*—a mirage! The cause of anxiety was not removed. We were still at the beginning almost of our task. We had achieved a point, gained a footing, for the moment, to be sure. We had earned comparative security. It was something to have got so far and reached the paddy. In case of a gale now we might haul up our boat on land and ourselves take shelter in one of the villages on shore. That was all, however; we could not travel much inland. We could not, for example, foot it all the way to Comillah or Agartala, if we wished to do so. For, though we had gained *terra firma*, we were not yet on the main land. The voyage across remained to be accomplished, by a good deal. After poling half an hour through the grassy margin of these villages, we again emerged in the open sea as it were. Now for the first time we realised our situation and awoke from our dream of security. The substantial and high bank on our right, dotted with prosperous-looking houses of the peasantry, was only a *Chur*—one of the numerous islands in this inland sea called the Megna river. More than one such tantalise the voyager before his anxieties are over and his flight from bank to bank can be finished. For our part, we were still at the mercy of the river, and must thread the mazes of the Megna for some hours more to come near the true shore opposite.

This is the invariable story of the navigation of the Megna, consequent upon the topographic peculiarities of the river. These extensive islands, peopled by a thriving tenantry with their substantial dwellings, were once fields of well-defined land, comparatively high and dry for raising jute or mustard, and these jute tracts themselves were originally low lands fit for only rice cultivation, being a good deal under water during the wet season and scarcely above at any other period, while the mere rice-lands commenced as sand-banks—dangerous shoals habitually hid in shallow stream but occasionally, in mid-summer, peeping through the river and being for the most part on a level with the encompassing element By gradual accretion, these sands turn to low holms—*Churs*, as they are called—firm enough for cultivation of one kind and then of another, until they reach the dignity of veritable islands fit for permanent habitation.

Such a journey cannot possibly be rich in incident. Unless one is lost and saved in a storm, there is nothing stirring to relate. The routine of daily life is the same on land and water—at least inland water, or riverine. Yet, there is a minor or an occasional difference. A trifling point may, perhaps, be stated, giving a glimpse of life on board river craft.

Every body knows the complaint of Coleridge's Mariner, or at least the lines—

> Water, water, everywhere,
> Nor any drop to drink.

The grievance, however, was not peculiar, being the lot of all maritime adventurers who do not take in a stock of spring water or who run out their stock. We inland voyagers have usually an advantage in this respect, our course lying through drinkable liquid. Nevertheless, we are not without our sorrows. Will it be believed that in a country like Bengal, a man might starve through the most populous districts unless he had taken care to provide himself with the commonest necessaries of life? The markets are few and far between—for instance, there are none between Baidyabazar and Bhoyrubbazar—and at any of them you must not expect anything—even rice. We, of course, had laid in our store of provisions and fuel. But we depended upon our exertions on the way and on our luck for fish and milk, both which we must have fresh or not at all. Now, fancy, in a rural country like this, there was no milk, and on the breast of a river, no fish !—at least for us. Yes, it was a regular case of Fish, fish, everywhere, but not a bit of small fry to eat. Tantalus could scarcely have been more sorely tempted and disappointed, thought I, in the pangs of famine of a Bengali, whose meat is milk and fish. Tantalus is a myth, though, whereas the Baboo crying for fish in vain in the midst of abundance, is a sad reality, daily and hourly repeated! We continually passed uncovered skiffs and canoes, long and short, with the crews watching in patience or more actively engaged. These wherries have a family likeness—their purpose was stamped on their faces as it were. Fishing? Why, fishing they all were, together or separately, but for any good we might derive from them, they seemed to have this exercise simply to have a little play. We offered to purchase—to no purpose! Our eloquence was wasted—we charmed without the slightest effect. It was all the same whether we asked in gentleness or demanded in distress or injured innocence. We entreated, we prayed. Even the never-failing blessing of the Brahman—son of Bharadwaj Rishi and Swyambhuva Manu himself—died on the breeze without reducing to terms the obdurate fishing heart. To the orthodox mind, this were evidence conclusive of our having strayed beyond the Aryan Pale. Surely, we had reached an Infidel land. The Megna is, indeed, a *parvenu* stream, however bloated with its newly-acquired wealth of waters. It is certainly not recognised in our Scriptures. The Brahmaputra—the old channel of which we passed yesterday—is the Eastern limit of Hindu civilization. The Hindu population of these parts are the descendants of adventurers who either left their country for their country's good or settled among the aboriginal tribes in quest of excitement or fortune. But, though the Hindus came first, the

Mahomedans now outnumber them by far. Most of the fishermen are followers of the Prophet, if of god or man at all. In fact, they are dry Red Ferazees all. Nay, they must be Wahabees, rebels against the Queen and Brahma—unconscionable, conscienceless fellows who do not mind starving a good Brahman rather than exchange their small fry with silver!

I write strongly because I write without hesitation. We made an exhaustive experiment and found the phenomenon, real and general, throughout our course in East Bengal. We tried every boat we saw, far and near. The more distant fishers did not even deign to answer. The nearer ones had not yet caught any fish. That was the stock story. And a cock-and-bull story it was, in many cases, beyond mistake! We suspected fish in the covered baskets. Our men of the upper deck or roof actually espied fish in the holds of some boats. But *cui bono?* The distant craft would not draw near—the nearer craft, with crafty glibness, solemnly protested their innocence of any fish *in esse*.

This phenomenon is not the trifle that gentlemen living in comfort and luxury in town might consider it. I do not so much mind my own martyrdom. But, surely, it is not fair to travellers in the country, specially to the voyagers through its numerous rivers, that they should starve, by being deprived of the ordinary meat of their table. A people living on fish, ought to have opportunities for buying fish even on their travels, at any rate in populous districts. Nor is the difficulty insurmountable. There are fish enough, but not for sale. Not that there is any real indisposition to sell. The regular fishers—the fishers in earnest—all fish for sale, working for a living, in part at least. Many of them no doubt pretend that they fish only for their own domestic consumption, but it is a mere pretence. Certainly, the reality might be tested by competition. Even those who really fish for their own table, might be induced by high prices for a scarce produce to give up a part of the yield of their operations. High prices—and travellers are disposed to pay fancy prices for the nonce for a luxury and much more for a necessary—might draw men from other pursuits to fishing in these rivers. But so long as the article is not forthcoming, there is no opportunity for competition. Whence, then, this hide-and-seek with a fruit of industry? This conduct is the more inexplicable when it is known that these fishermen, most of them, take their fish to the neighbouring markets on land. Why don't they sell off on the river? The cause is simple enough. The whole is a question of efficient administration. The Government is to blame, as in so many other matters. The fact is that the poor fishermen are not protected. Not that they have been deliberately outlawed, but they are virtually at the mercy of the strong and evil-disposed. Oppressed in the middle of a great river, they must pocket the wrong as well as they can. The vast waters are no doubt the highways of commercial and social intercourse, but in their very vastness and solitude they constitute a desert. Who is there to shield the feeble against the mighty? Whom can the fishers look up to for redress? The court is far off, the Police station is not near, and the Police themselves are a terror—to the poor and lowly. Under any circumstances, information laid at the Police station does not remove the necessity of complaining in court. The pursuit of justice entails expense and causes delay and trouble and anxiety, and is altogether too much of a luxury for the poor fishers. They do not see the wisdom of spending five pound ten to purchase the satisfaction of bringing to court a man who may have forcibly taken away without payment a shilling's worth of shrimps. For, after all, the man might slip through the fingers of justice! Law, always a troublesome and uncertain game, is doubly, quadruply, troublesome and uncertain a pursuit for them. Those who know anything of courts will recognise at once how hard it is for fishermen on the great rivers to bring the plunderers of their fish to book, through the established machinery. So there is practically a *carte blanche* to the high hand. Hence their nervous dread of all powerful customers as ugly customers. They secrete their draughts and deny possession of fish for the same reason that, in times of Mahratta or other lawlessness, the people buried their treasure and put on the appearance of poverty. The fishermen look tremulously askance at all large and well-manned craft, but they are in mortal terror of the great pinnaces, *bhaulias* and *koshes.* These are the worst Mahrattas—marauders, that is. A solitary fishing dingy with two men in it, is completely at the mercy of a big boat with a numerous crew. Even the larger fishing vessels are no match for these boats of prey. Still they may show some fight in defence of their own. When they can, they run away, but generally it is impossible for them to leave their situation. It is when the pinnaces and barges carry passengers, specially lordly Europeans, that they become all-devouring whales. Exceptions no doubt there are—large exceptions. There are just and humane men, watchful of their servants, who permit no wrong either in their own name or on their people's account. But the generality of Europeans leave matters very much to their servants. They are too absorbed to know all that passes about them and too high to enquire how the *hilsa* for their table on board is obtained. How their attendants and guards and camp-followers obtain theirs, is, of course, none of *their* business. They may have an eye for the picturesque and an ear for Mozart or Verdi, but they commonly fail in patience with sights and sounds of distress and could scarcely recognise them if they would. They have no time for trifles involving an occasional extortion or a little plunder of mere fish from naked men fishing on the way. Nor can they be approached for complaint.

The inaccessibility of European gentlemen of every degree, official and unofficial, is, indeed, the despair of suffering natives. Hence the terror with which the European is regarded. His presence in the rural districts causes a general unrest. It is the signal for the people to look out. They eye his cavalcade or Kafila with suspicion—watch his manners and movements from a distance or on tiptoe, ready to "bolt" away. Not till he and his myrmidons are fairly out of their neighbourhood, can they be well at ease. For, they may any moment be deprived of their own without ceremony, or their things used without their consent, or themselves impressed as porters or labourers without regard to their convenience or social status. Their "honor"—*izzat*—is clearly in peril, from the propinquity of the Saheb. The more experienced villages may even be deserted at the advent—the shops closed, the carts disabled, the draught cattle dispersed—only a lot of curious urchins and old women, interspersed with a few begging cripples and blind men, being left behind to give reception fit to his White Majesty. Of course, the Saheb knows not all this, nor understands. Reading the above account, well might he exclaim much as Warren Hastings did at the end of one of Burke's orations in the Impeachment: He never suspected that he was such a monster of iniquity! In truth, his men commit him sadly. They make him a curse to the poor, where he might himself be disposed to be a blessing. But he cannot be altogether absolved. It is his duty to see and hear for himself, so far as possible, and, above all, to keep strict watch over servants and understrappers. The neglect of that prime duty involves him in sin, as it plunges the people in misery.

That goes far to account for the attitude of the fishermen on the Megna and other rivers. They are simply afraid of plunder. And not without cause. In fact, they have learnt by bitter experience what they have to expect from the large fleets and the big boats. They will not confess to having succeeded in catching fish—they will not even come near to give you a chance of searching in their baskets and the holds of their vessels. Of course, it is the natives that suffer chiefly for want of fish, which is their staff of life. But the evil is not confined to one article or to the water only. If the Europeans were not well provided from beforehand, they might feel with their darker fellow-subjects. What is true in regard to fish and fishermen on the river, is true of fowls and eggs and milk and other provisions and fuel on the banks, more or less. The retail trade along the whole course of the rivers has been hurt, by the dread of the larger boats used by Europeans and the more respectable natives, to the distress of innocent wayfarers, specially if travelling with some attendance and in comfort. And here I am bound to say that some Baboos are quite as bad for neglect and heartless indifference as any Sahebs—several even worse. For Many Europeans would pay liberally if they knew how to reach the people, for the masters are fleeced all the same whether the purchases are adequately paid for or not; but some Baboos, I am afraid, take advantage of the opportunity for taking things at their own prices, if not for wholesale plundering.

I have already dwelt on the difficulty of provisioning on the way, and specially noticed the strange fish famine in the midst of abundance to which the voyager on these rivers is exposed. And I have recorded the true cause. These great boats used chiefly by the Sahebs—Europeans, high Government officers, planters and so forth —are the terror of the lonely fishermen, in twos or threes, plying their trying pursuit. The poor fellows are simply afraid of being made victims of plunder.

I noticed this remarkable shyness, of a far from shrinking class, in all my previous voyages to the East. This time too I have remarked that the crew of all three of my boats as well as my own people made the greatest efforts to obtain fish. They offered tempting prices, but the men would not approach. Although myself involved with the rest, I could only cry—Served them right! This, in fine, is the Nemesis of *zooloom!* Only the innocent like myself suffer with the guilty—that's the pity of it!

The uncommitted Hindu who has not yet had an opportunity of compromising his caste by measuring the ocean, feels himself sufficiently at sea in these unusually broad rivers of his native country, whose one bank cannot always be seen from the other bank, and the crossing of which cousumes often the greater part of a day. In the Megna specially, which at its grander curves is more an inland sea than a river, he has a consciousness of maritime adventure. All the moving incidents by flood and field he may have read or heard of, come to mind. In particular the Poets of the sea are remembered, from Shakespeare down to Falconer. One naturally muses on the classic lyrics of Campbell and the homelier songs of Dibdin. Byron's grand apostrophe to the Mediterranean, of course, comes to the lips—

Roll on, thou deep and dark blue ocean—roll !
Ten thousand fleets sweep over thee in vain ;
Man marks the earth with ruin—his control
Stops with the shore ;—upon the watery plain
The wrecks are all thy deed, nor doth remain
A shadow of man's ravage, save his own,
When, for a moment, like a drop of rain,
He sinks into thy depths with bubbling groan,
Without a grave, unknell'd, uncoffin'd, and unknown.

* * * *

Thou glorious mirror, where the Almighty's form
Glasses itself in tempests ; in all time,
Calm or convuls'd—in breeze, or gale, or storm,
Icing the pole, or in the torrid clime
Dark-heaving ;—boundless, endless, and sublime—
The image of eternity—the throne
Of the Invisible ; even from out thy slime
The monsters of the deep are made ; each zone
Obeys thee ; thou goest forth, dread, fathomless, alone.

As leaving our shelter at the mouth of the

Minakhali we launched out into the Amazonian river and was fairly in the middle of the Megna, I exclaimed in the autobiographic lines with which the same Bard opens the third canto of his Pilgrimage, in the character of Harold:—

> Once more upon the waters! yet once more!
> And the waves bound beneath me as a steed
> That knows his rider. Welcome, to their roar!
> Swift be their guidance, wheresoe'er it lead!
> Though the strain'd mast should quiver as a reed,
> And the rent canvas fluttering strew the gale,
> Still must I on; for I am as a weed,
> Flung from the rock, on ocean's foam, to sail
> Where'er the surge may sweep, the tempest's breath prevail.

I have already described the cut across the Megna, with the succession of isles and islets, inhabited, uninhabited, and uninhabitable, and of broad tracts and small patches of cultivation, some on dry land and others more or less submerged, in the bosom of the stream. We are now on the left bank—not exactly *on*, nor even very *close to*, the bank, for a great sand-bank under cultivation intervenes. We are, however, on the Tipperah side, and feel a good deal relieved on that account.

Reaching the verge of the sand-bank in question, we take advantage of a favorable breeze to stick up our masts and unfurl our sails. We sweep through the paddy fields under water, between large tracts of jute cultivation, all in the bed of the great river, making in our course a fine whistling, wheezing noise, most soothing to the sense. Then we plunge into deeper water to catch the breeze and career through it proudly to a grander accompaniment of the music of the rolling element. Not without a conscious sense of danger, however, for the sky is overcast, clouds hover about us overhead, the waves are bounding not violently yet, but ominously enough, and we find ourselves all alone in the sea of waters, which in a few minutes might assume another and still more frowning aspect, and prove too much for our skill and resources. The very haze of the far off drizzle before us, making sky and water of one consistency as it were, affrights the mariner's soul. There certainly can be no mistake about the import of our isolation. While other boats in large caravans are huddled together pining in inaction at some rural port, or perhaps starving in some lonely creek, biding their time for a clear sky, we are the only rash fellows to tempt the terrible genius of the boat-devouring river—Megna the Cut-throat, as it is popularly called. For we are not yet safe. Not near enough to be able to run up shore at the signal of trouble, we are at the mercy of a sudden squall.

We are cutting through the water at a fine rate. At half past eleven in the forenoon, we are overtaken by rain. In half an hour breakfast is announced. It is breakfast to be sure, as we have tasted no morsel since last evening; but it may be called dinner as well, for its importance. Nay, for that matter, our first and last meal in day-time, as one of our two in the whole twenty-four hours, this mid-day eating is our breakfast, luncheon and dinner all in one. For all that, even under the best conditions, it would not be much of a thing in European estimation. There is usually variety enough and the sensible proportions are respectable, yet the able-bodied up-countryman would, in a few mouthfuls, make a clean sweep of the whole thing ; the British Rakshasa would simply starve on it. The ordinary Hindu diet is simplicity itself. The poetry of Reginald Heber has familiarised even English society at Home with the idea.

The Hindu cooks his simple food,—

sings the good Bishop. Now, this simplicity obliges the Hindu to be ready for his repast as soon as it is prepared. Cold meat is not usually a delicacy, but a shoulder or leg of mutton—we shudder to name the other thing so dear to Old John Bull !—will stand a deal of neglect or coldness. Procrastination, however, is the thief of vegetable flavour. A non-animal dish soon ceases to be edible. Cooked farina are best eaten warm from the fire. We are well provided with Bombay mangoes and other fruits and sweetmeats from Dacca as well as with rice, flour, dal, ghee, oil, spices, vegetables, &c. Nevertheless, our fare is poor even for Bengalis, in the absence of the only two animal elements, (and they are the prime elements) of fish and milk. It is all the more necessary not to allow our rice to rot and our curries to vegetate with a vengeance in our cooking shed afloat. The rain, however, is beating our little barks mercilessly. It were foolish to wait for close of a shower in its season. So we have the cooking boat brought alongside of the flag-boat, and direct our Brahman *Chef* to hand over all at once our plates and dishes of victuals for our table, under cover of napkins and towels, from that boat to us in ours through one shutter which is opened for the purpose.

After our breakfast, the rain is over, and at 1 O'clock the boats put up sail, and by 3 P.M. we stop at the first entrance to the Teetas for the other boats to come up. The broad canvas of our vessel giving it an advantage over our smaller and lighter craft, we have come far ahead, and could have gone farther still but for the fear they might lose their way among the many outlets at the junction with the tributary. This at all events is a plausible excuse for a halt to which our men are the more inclined, having in two hours made an ordinary day's journey. But we won't let them waste the remainder of the day, so we start again, poling slowly away through the shallow creek. Meanwhile, the other boats have joined the flag boat, and Ishan Manji, the commander of the cook-boat, who is so familiar with the routes to this part of Tipperah, being continuously engaged in plying between Dacca and Agartala, takes the lead, piloting us. After a deal of dull plodding through paddy half under water, we enter something like a rivulet.

A distinct difference in vegetation is observable The palm thrives not even in North Dacca.

Here we altogether miss the towering chiefs of Oriental botany. There are no cocoanuts, and *Tal* is a strange sound in these parts. Not even the graceful areca, with its tall, slender, elastic figure crowned by copious foliage like a beautiful head of hair, which charmed us all the way up to Sonargong, is discoverable. The bamboo pursues us still but in neglected groves, and altogether there is a wilder look in the botany. The Shaora *(Trophis aspersa)*, a fine forest tree of a wiry substantial-looking trunk with a knotty disposition and a dull moss color, and with substantial, beautiful little leaves of a deep blue green color and a circular form, is by no means unknown around Calcutta, but it is getting scarce everyday, of course. It is common in the Dacca woods, and abounds on the banks of this creek or arm, or rather finger of the Megna, as it appears after all.

The Jugya Doomboor *(Ficus glomerata)*, the wild Java plum (*Eugenia Jambulana)*, and the Gambir, recur as often as the bamboo, more than the wild or Dal Karamcha. There is another common tree called Hijol (*Barringtonia acutangula*), from whose branches descend numerous green pendants of green-colored berries. Perhaps the most curious is the Boroon, vulgarly Borné (*Capparis trifoliata*), of the size of small Gambirs, loaded with a fruit of the size of the peach but of dull coarse green. The leaf is like that of the Bengal blackberry called Jam (Hindi, *Jamun.*) In copying from my Diary, my clerk, a native of the Megna valley, informs me that the tree derives its name from Varuna, the Lord of Waters, from its growing at the water's edge or in the bed of streams. I plucked some bunches to see, and found the fruits irregularly round, strong and heavy, and taking no pressure of the fingers. They were still far from ripe, but from the way in which the tree grows in neglected profusion they are evidently of no use—except as a ready substitute for brick-bats—to pelt the enemy with—in a land without brick or stone. I imagine they are never softer than I found them. Cattle avoid them.

I believe the Boroon fruit and bark will on trial disclose medical properties. After nightfall, the branches I had plucked emitted a strong disagreeable smell, in so much that we were obliged to throw them away at a distance—an indication of constitutional acridity. Whether cultivation might improve the Boroon fruit into an edible, is problematical. But I can scarcely think so much abundance of Nature to be meant for nothing. Meanwhile at any rate, the trees make a good diversion in the prospect of the bank with their swarming pendants oscillating in the breeze right over the water. I say bank only, because on our immediate left are long strips of alluvion full of paddy or jute. There is water beyond and alluvion again and then water and so on, to the far off firm bank of the stream. I may here note that Durga Prosad Gupta mentioned to Kumad Nath a fruit in the Kailashahar hills one side of which is sweet and wholesome to eat and the other side—death! Kumad Nath has not seen it, Durga Prosad tried to procure for his inspection a fruit at Agartala, where this conversation took place, but without success. Durga Prosad had heard that it grew also in the hills in the neighbourhood of Agartala. These trees, with the Dal Karamcha, Hijol, and others of good leafage and stems, would be an acquisition to the botany of the down country. The continual recurrence of these trees in crowds, mingled with the graceful bamboo, makes a charming prospect on yonder bank. Yet there are many well-known things of beauty in the vegetable kingdom wanting. I cannot help comparing the vegetation here with the botany of the country higher up as well as with that of my own district in metropolitan Bengal. The vegetation on this bank approximates to that at Agartala, without being half so rich. Here the Jewul *(Odina Wodier)* is the common fencing tree around habitations. At Agartala, not only the Jewul but also the

Kurchi (*Echites antidysenterica*) and other like trees are used for the purposes of fencing and fuel. I see no mangoes or jacks about here. They are common enough in Agartala. There, too, we have the cultivated Champa (*Michelia Champaka*), Nageswar (*Mesua ferrea*), and the secluded and luxuriant Kantali Champa. Last, not least, I miss here the Shimool (*Bombax heptaphyllum*)—the great silk cotton tree—which is as common in Deltaic Bengal as in the Tipperah hills. It is a plant that will compare with any in the world for stately grandeur and brilliancy of flower. I once got from the forest in the interior of the Tipperah Hills a curious colossal wild almond. I call it almond because the kernel has the almond taste. The pod is like a big case containing lots of edible seed or kernel enclosed in different cells separated from one another by paper-like walls. I carried several of these pods to Calcutta to present them to Dr. King of the Botanical Gardens, but did not do so, and they went to rot in my house.

Entering this creek or arm of the Megna or mouth of the Teetas, we came first upon a village mart held in the open at a place called Murchakandi. The appearance was unmistakable, though it was not market day (the *hât* taking place on Sundays), and there were only one or two little boats then. In about an hour more we reached a busier and far more important place called Ulookandi, where there were a number of substantial-looking thatched houses in the midst of trees and a good number of boats, some of them of heavy tonnage. We moor for the night a little beyond, in the neighbourhood, at the mouth of a narrow rill, in which we may easily take shelter on any sudden stress of weather. It is not dark yet, and we might push a little way higher up, but there is no safe or comfortable anchorage, as our sailors averred, within attainable distance. Besides, it is necessary to avoid the vicinity of jungle or of sites where the harvested jute plant is undergoing rotting under water, if we are to escape the attacks of the mosquito host. The rotting jute in especial emits a horrid stink reminding one of chemical abominations like bromium.

After all, it is not a very safe place. The banks of the Megna are noted as the haunts of pirates. The ominous-named Chorepara cannot be far off. As I am writing, my valet Lakir hurries up to report that the boatmen warn us to be on the alert. He proposes to fire a few blank cartridges by way of notice to the robbers to expect a warm reception. I am not in the least alarmed, being fully prepared to meet any local loafers. I scout the danger to cheer up my fellows. Kumud Nath tries to reassure Lakir by reminding him of the numerous boats in our neighbourhood at Ulookandi. Lakir still whines that those boats are a good way off —though they are almost within a stone's throw. So I interpose, saying that we are ourselves a whole fleet. We have our Sepoys besides, and my stalwart orderly Pitambar Singh, whom the neighbouring villagers have seen in his thundering Panjabi *pagri*, is a host himself. Sir Valet reminds me that though I have men, I am not provided with much of an arsenal and magazine—the Tipperah sepoys themselves, come to escort me, though in uniform, having left their arms behind, to escape the inquisition of the British Indian Arms Act. He proposes to arm Pitambar with my gun, leaving me and my friend my two swords between us. This being agreed to, he says that the whole fleet will be ill at ease unless a *feu de—peur* is fired. I acquiesce. Thereupon he gives aloud the word of command to Pitambar Singh ; after finishing his cooking and eating, he is to discharge a few volleys.

Saturday, 26th July.—He tried, but in vain. The gun, a good rifle, present of the Maharaja in my first voyage to Tipperah, has been a good Brahman's weapon ever since my last trip. Rusting in the family house at Baranagar, it has been brought with us as the only chance of saving it from imminent ruin. The attempt to utilise it in its fresh career of active service, was not very promising. Notwithstanding all the manipulation of my big orderly and the lesser fellows and all the ministrations of my servant, the gun would not go off. At night, besides the *bearer* at the *punka*, I directed the orderly Pitambar Singh to keep watch. Two sepoys were to do likewise, by turns, one watching while the other slept, and give alarm at the approach of danger. The arrangement was superfluous, however, so far as keeping some one awake was concerned. For, I myself had scarcely a wink of sleep, in consequence of a strong cup of coffee. The Orissian part of my retinue, too, appears to have been much too frightened for rest. At least the *bearer* who was to relieve the man at the *puuka* was wide-awake. Perceiving a movement of the boat, his worst suspicions were roused. He had been told that dacoits often stealthily cut the ropes and slowly and imperceptibly lead the boat down the stream to a convenient solitude at a distance, away from possibility of help, the better to execute their purpose. So he got up on the roof and called to the cook in the cook's boat. I heard him, but was too comfortable and too little ruffled to enquire, though my ears were all attention to note if there were any symptoms of danger. Kumud Nath, however, was startled out of his repose, and rushed out to see what was the matter. He found my grenadier and the other sentry fast asleep, the former ensconced in a corner of the servants' room, and the latter stretched at full length on the deck. When, however, the disturbance roused them, the sepoy had the impudence to protest that he had been keeping up the whole night, and went the length of pretending that at the time Kumud Baboo got up, he was conversing with his up-country fellows—at a respectable distance from one another, it must have been, though! And to add to his guilt and prove his stupidity, he charged with neglect the very alarm-giving Orissian who, according to orders, might have been sleeping without reproach till his turn came to relieve the *punka-man*, but who was really not only awake but the most truthful of all my followers. It proved to be a needless alarm, nonetheless praise is due to the man who would have been the cause of our safety had there come any real danger.

This morning I rose at dawn to rouse the sailors. They were up already, but dilly-dallying, after their manner. At the sound of my voice, Kumud Nath got up, though visibly drowsy still. I could not help feeling somewhat ashamed of disturbing him so early, specially after the incident in the small hours ; but as he joined me in right earnest in calling the crew to be quick in starting, I felt reassured, and when next he proceeded to open up the shutters, I said by way of offering consolation, that we might go to sleep again, after having seen our fleet under weigh.

We proceeded to enter the Teetas proper as we thought, but there was no such thing. Again and again we were deceived. We thought we were already in the Teetas, but were soon compelled to abandon that flattering delusion. Where, then, were we? The Lord only knows! The water through which our course ran scarcely constituted a great river, so far as we could see. Still less had it the appearance of the Megna—it was not anything half or quarter so broad. But it is the Megna—the little Megna, you are assured. And surely it is broad enough for that matter. But there is no knowing. We have been half-a-dozen times in and out of the Megna and half-a-dozen times in and out of the Teetas, till we begin to fear we are in neither, nor near either! We cannot answer for the integrity of our brains under the strain. Ever on the move, we cannot say we are in a fix, but in the mazes of this liquid labyrinth, we are truly in a puzzle. Our consciousness of identity still remains, but that of locality has been unsettled. We are a continual Miss in motion. But there is no help for it. None seems to be acquainted with the geography of the quarter. Our Dacca navigators themselves, who are understood to have often plied their oars in these waters, are quite at sea. The natives are stupid or mute. One venerable Moslem gives it the name of Sooti, but before we can enjoy the relief of having got something definite, the fellow, as if correcting himself, adds—"Sooti of the Megna." Oh the horrid bore! the everlasting Megna! Enough! Enough! The "sweetest honey is loathsome" by—surfeit, and there may be too much of even the noble Megna!

Jolly Youth contradicts crabbed Age. A boy whom we meet with fishing promptly says, "This is the Pagla Nadi." Right for once! right beyond question! our jaded hearts instinctively declared. Whatever the merits of the old controversy between youth and age, whether the advantage usually lies with childhood or adolescence, whether the Boy of the Period or his grandfather is the true booby, certain it is that this home-bred stripling has spoken the truth about the matter—given the right name to the right thing. This simple hamlet boy has justly characterised this distressing and distracting piece of water—this mysterious stream! Pagla, to be sure! Pagla, and no mistake! By all means Pagla! If water can lose its senses, here is the phenomenon! If a river can go mad, this stream is undoubtedly a stark lunatic!

I believe the poor boy is literally and unfiguratively true. Indeed, I think I remember having seen the name in the Surveyor General's map of this District. And the name befits the thing, in more respects than one. Wayward in the extreme, now it broadens into a vast expanse, now it contracts, till it loses itself in an insignificant channel between two small villages. Here, once more, is a regular Indian Deltaic river, winding before us into what would be regarded a grand reach in England! Above us to our left, on the opposite bank, we espy a rural port or market-place with the unmistakable ranges of sheds, close to an important hamlet to its left extending in a pretty long strip along the bank. We ask our pilot Ishan Manji the name of the *hat.* He either does not know and evades, or simply tells the truth, that it is a new thing, adding that not to know it did not argue one's self ignorant. Pursuing the enquiry, I get from one of a group of villagers the name of Moolar Hat. Moola, I believe, is Moollah or Mollah, a Mahomedan priest. Hence it is the Mollah's market from belonging to a Mahomedan Padre.

We have by no means given up the enquiry into the identity of the water we are measuring. Our perseverance is Teutonic. One calls it the Tishna and then the Tishta. Are we really coming to Darjeeling, after all? Why, some fine morning we may awake on the Nile, or for that matter, on the Thames, in the course of this more than Nearchean Periplus! There is nothing so absurd as ignorance. Ignorance pure and simple, ignorance thick and impenetrable, is equal to any nonsense. The men mean, of course, the Teetas, but call it by the other names *par excellence*. They respect their river too much to call it by its vulgar appellation of Teetas, but essay to round it off into something different and somewhat less common. They Sanskritise the name, as in Europe they might Latinise it, and get the absurd result —"Tishna" or "Tishta." Poor fellows! they only copy their betters. Poor fellows! they only want instruction.

Name or no name, we proceed onwards. And now another at another village on the bank declares, without circumlocution or pseudo-classicism, it is the Teetas. Blessed unanimity! But it is really getting too serious for irony. Would to God our bumpkin were a true prophet! It is trying enough to be dragging our slow length along; but then, not to know our way, in a tortuous system of water—to advance with might and main without the assurance of progress,—this is abominable!

Verily, it seems as if the offended genius of the element is leading us through a watery maze. What length of fluid have we passed! what tedious turns have we taken, since the early dawn! And yet not to have reached the Teetas, seems a marvel! To the traveller panting to reach his destination as quickly as may be, it is a torture. Yesterday was better passed. We were in high spirits from having made a remarkably quick passage of the most important part of the journey, for the sailing through the Dacca river is a mere introductory to the voyage in earnest. Notwithstanding our venturing across the Megna against the inclination and audible protest of the commanders and sailors, we had had a safe flight athwart and a prosperous voyage. We congratulated ourselves on our good luck. We had crossed our Rubicon and were within measurable distance of our Rome. We had "done" the Megna at all events—the rest was plain sailing. If we had not seen the Nabinagar temple (near the confluence of the

Megna and the Teetas), in the same way the Maheshardi temple (in the vicinity of Baidya-bazar) escaped us; but there could be no mistake about our progress. In fact, last evening we were not only sure we had left Nabinager a good way behind, but we thought we were taking the shorter cut through the Buldakhal Pargana, avoiding the waters in the neighbourhood of Nabinagar promontory, and never expecting to catch any glimpse of its famous landmark, the steeple. How we were mistaken! What was our surprise this morning to behold the old temple! But we not only see it, we do nothing else almost! We see it again and again—and over again and once more, and yet not for the last time! It holds on to us with a firm grip, and scarcely ever permits us out of sight. In vain we bid it farewell, we return to it, notwithstanding all the way we proceed. We are in a pretty predicament, with this movable fixture of a steeple. A vague feeling creeps upon us. Is the moss-grown temple the seat of a sinister spirit? Is our fleet haunted? or are we mad? Certainly at each remove we do not even draw a lengthening chain. The chain lessens and enlarges, but it increases not to a satisfactory degree. At least, so soon as we fancy we are escaping the bonds, we are brought back to our senses and to the everlasting monument. Thus fettered like Andromeda as it were, and treated very like Tantalus, we pass and repass the steeple times without number. The steeple pursues us with inexorable malignity.

The intelligent passenger in the waters of Lower Bengal has his troubles enough. At every step he has to lament his geographical helplessness. Consigned to the uneducated and uncurious guidance of the native boatmen—themselves unarmed with map or chart or instrument of any kind, without even an ordinary compass, finding their way by a sort of instinct—by vague remembrance of straggling hamlets and sandbanks, more or less new and shifting—in a country without brick or wooden habitations, through rivers without a masonry or wooden landing-place, and not caring if in ignorance they doubled and trebled and quadrupled the same place and dodged about the same quarter a dozen times so long as their day's hire was safe—he is, to say the least, in a very unenviable frame of mind. It is bad enough that he does not know—he cannot make sure that his Captain is not hopelessly at sea. Although his boat is always on the move, yet, unable to recognise the course of his navigation, the voyager does not feel making any progress. Who knows that the boat is not, after all, sailing in a circle? There are no substantial land-marks—no handiwork of man or God—to lead the way. There is not even a diversity of scenery to afford materials for identification. Before and behind, above and around, all is unvarying prospect. The same monotony of low lands and water, attends at every step, oppressing the traveller and embarrassing the boatman.

After a hundred disappointments, we are again said to be in the Teetas. It is—it is—the Teetas, my soul! The Teetas and no mistake!—I see it—I feel it.—We have been done for, however. The tension on the spirits has been too great. It is wearying, exasperating journey. But why come this way at all during this easy season, when the water god is so propitious? Why not make the short cut, through the heart of the British District of Tipperah? One is inclined to suspect the boatmen, who are paid per diem instead of by voyage, of prolonging the journey by leading us through the maze. Even in the absence of any motive for going astray, these Eastern sailors are a sufficiently vicious set. They will go their own way and pursue their own views, accepting no counsel even though manifestly to their advantage. They are the most imperturbable fellows in the world; you can never hope to reason with them, far less bring them over to your side. In general, they keep you at bay by their knowing stupidity.

They meet your frank kindly advances with cool *nonchalance*. They give vague exasperating answers to your most specific points. Finally, if you grow too importunate or energetic, they have their own recipe for it —a moral wet blanket: They are simply unconquerably mute!

We came upon a goodly village of prosperous jute cultivators called, in the usual uncertainty about the geography of these parts, Bhola or Oola. In fact, the whole tract on our right is a settlement of well-to-do jute rayyets. In the country below, the paddy is half above water and the plant far too young, while the jute in general is more or less ripe for harvest. Occasionally some fields have been cut, but very few. As we go up, we see greater progress. There is more active harvesting and dipping. Last afternoon we passed through a good deal of stinking water, stinking from action of jute steeped in it. Towards, and in, the Teetas, the season is evidently more advanced. There is still much jute standing, a good deal still immature, yet a considerable quantity has been cut and dipped, some of it already skinned, and some even dried and ready and being sent to market as veritable jute of commerce. The women show unmistakable sign of circulation of coin among the people. They sport precious white metal in almost all limbs—solid silver ornaments—the goodly-sized anklets, and sets of bracelets (churi), the wide stiff neck-belt, together with other and lighter neck-chains of different kinds—all pure silver. The jewellery is, of course, more substantial than pretty. Even in substance they fall much below the standard towards Calcutta. In so far, it must be confessed, the rural damsels of the East have the advantage in taste. The jewel of their lower extremities is, of course, the twisted anklet peculiar to East Bengal. On the other hand, I have not yet discovered in these parts the massive leg-cuffs which our ladies were wont to prize and to enjoy on their fair nether limbs.

The women on this voyage are all ill-favored ugly creatures. At one house I pointed out to Kumud a fairish, perhaps fair (according to this country) girl, holding a child on her hip, and a darker beauty of maturer years who looked at us with such eyes, and who had such a figure!

Perhaps the most interesting sight during our voyage, was reserved for us in the afternoon. After threading through the endless mazes of this liquid labyrinth—variously denominated Pagla and Sooti—of the Megna creek or the mouth of the Teetas, we came upon a goodly little stream in the middle of wide fields of paddy, diversified by occasional plots of jute. A lighter breeze swept over us, essaying to smooth our way up the adverse current, but the effort of Eolus failed from the weight of our large lumbering craft. It was, however, only necessary to spread our canvas to assist the views or disposition of the God of wind. Even this moderate measure of self-help the boatmen did not show. Nay, they wilfully withheld it. They would not take the trouble to set up the mast and fit up the single simple sail, even to save themselves the much greater trouble of poling up. All our suggestions and advice and even demonstration were unavailing. Entreaty was tried next with no better result and then threats were resorted to. I should say *threat*, for the mild Hindoo could in conscience hold out but one—against the pockets, namely. We would mulct them for this insane policy—this wilful delay; on settling day at end of our journey, they would repent of it when too late. Had we preached to the winds half as eloquently, we might have produced a better impression; we should at least have got an answer. These tyrants of the rivers seemed to hear not. Like deaf and dumb they drudged on, without making any progress, until they were fairly tired themselves, and then, of their own accord, they quietly brought up their rag from its hiding-place in the hold, and, with it, fitted up the mast which they raised, after having wasted so much valuable time. The effect was instantaneous. It seemed as if new life was infused into the heavy bark. It was a pleasant sight to see the vessel cutting through the water with a will, yet with perfect ease. Still they had put up only a small minor sail, as if by a compromise between their obstinacy and their self interest. Pleasant too was it to behold the other boats running up to us from far behind and sweeping past us and ahead. In especial we watched some gigantic boats of the mercantile navy, laden from top to bottom, forcing up by very power of sail. The sails are puffed up like balloons ; like balloons, too, they seem to make for the upper sky—one almost expects the whole mercantile fleet to be every moment forced out of water, to go on a voyage through the air, after the lighter craft of æronauts ! And why not? If one kind of boat, why not another kind? It is only a question of motive power, and the force of wind is not to be despised. To my mind, boats of this description stand a good chance of leaving the beds of river to navigate the circumambient deep. I have always indulged this idea from boyhood when watching the traffic borne on the bosom of my native Hooghly. Happily, my apprehension has not been realised and will never be, for very good reasons. But so long as the sails of any vessels swell upward instead of forward, so long as they are propelled in a perpendicular rather than a horizontal direction, it is impossible always to avoid being anxious on their account. The cause of imaginary fear may, after all, be cause of genuine safety. The boats in question are so mercilessly laden whenever opportunity occurs, that they are sunk in water to the neck and ears; a slight movement —a breath—seems sufficient to complete the plunge, overwhelming boat and cargo and all. It is obviously an advantage to such craft, when the wind is high, to be artificially borne up above the waves by the peculiar disposition of canvas. Here I observed that, at the next turn of the river, the sails of all the boats fluttered in the breeze as from irritation at the change of direction. This flutter might be dangerous to boats scarcely raised above the water, but for the upward tendency of their sails.

Proceeding thus some way, we come upon a vast marsh now all under water, more or less, sown all over with paddy half emerged, except in the middle where the water is always too deep for cultivation. Our boat is led into this marsh. They evidently purpose to cross it. They have at length given up their minor canvas and hoisted up the major. And now thoroughly equipped under full sail, we cut right through this great level. It is a magnificent sight and a grand sensation! I think of all manner of enjoying travel; but nothing comes up to the mark. Camel-driving in the desert is an infliction at best. Riding 'cross country is far pleasanter, but the back of a horse is far from an easy-chair. Why, caparisoned elephant bearing canopied throne, moving mightily through the boundless prairie, would be poor frolic in comparison to our journey now! There is nothing in the universe equal to this boat-riding 'cross country in Rural Bengal! We sweep proudly with a sublime music through the far-spreading rich velvet carpet of emerald, now rolling along the waving expanse of the never-ending long grass which feeds the cattle of the country, now stemming the stouter and more loudly musical resistance of the later jute cultivation, and anon shooting athwart the lake in the centre, through the sea of whistling paddy, ever and ever more with an increasing sense of infinity!

At last we were overtaken by rain and wind. It was a ceaseless torrent beating mercilessly against our poor fleet. The scene was indescribably animated. The concert of the elements deafened yet charmed us, as with a grand overture of Nature herself. But now the groans of Eolus were heard far above the roar of ths liquid accompaniment. We had been uncomfortable already from the violent invasion of the rain penetrating to the hitherto air-and-water-tight saloon of the flagboat, and far into the snuggest retreats ; and now we became uneasy. A distinct anxiety seized the mind. While the poetry of Nature maintained itself, the drama of life deepened towards the *denoument* as it were. Undefined feelings of danger—vague terrors of wreck and ruin in the midst of the dreary moor, now a Mediterranean Sea, the lands whereof are undiscerned in the surrounding mist, where, wholly unprovided as we were with scientific aids, we had early lost our sense of the very cardinal points—invested this part of the voyage with a weird fascination in the imagination of the brave Baboo mariner who has no higher triumphs by flood or field in store for him. Indeed, it was a sufficiently ugly-looking business for any unprofessional stamina ; specially when the finishing touch was given. For, in this situation night fell upon the scene, before we were well out of our inland rice lake. Unable to see our way, not knowing which side to turn, we stopped, anchoring in the swamp now truly dismal. There we passed the night, the first part of it in fear of being lost and drowned, the rest, when the storm passed away, in imminent danger of being cut down and plundered by pirates.

Our Herculean guardsman of an orderly, Pitamber Sing, by way of apology for last night's neglect of duty and of escape from watching that night, sent up the boy Jogi as a messenger with a long tale of sickness and suffering from cholera or dysentery, having had forty motions every day. I was up at once to search among my chests for appropriate medicine, but Kumud Nath, with pretensions more peremptory than imperfect worldliness, would not let me. He said it was all nonsense, and he knew the man. Yet the man was ailing nevertheless, as I afterwards learnt, not having cooked since leaving Dacca and from before living on hard raw barley meal and gram, softened in cold water, seasoned with salt and chillies. So much for unsympathising shrewdness !

We took the usual precautions for our safety. Besides, I myself was in no hurry to go to sleep. Nor was it without interest to watch my little fleet riding at anchor in the undefined lake.

> Our boat is asleep on Serchio's stream,
> Its sails are folded like thoughts in a dream,
> The helm sways idly, hither and thither ;
> Dominic, the boat-man, has brought the mast,
> And the oars, and the sails ; but 'tis sleeping fast,
> Like a beast, unconscious of its tether.

For the contending gods of the elements, after a sharp skirmish which developed into the proportions and the seriousness of a regular battle, had made up their differences and were thenceforward content to live in peace and quiet. And even in the phenomena of external nature

> Peace hath her victories
> No less renowned than war.

For

> The poetry of earth is never dead.

Soon I had an opportunity of realising the truth of the Poet's address—

> Ye stars which are the poetry of the heaven !

Rain and storm subsided, the sky put on its robe of silk bespangled with golden flowers. And anon, the still loveliness of the surrounding scene beguiled the modest moon out of the screen, behind which, like a lady of the Orient, she had taken shelter earlier in the evening.

The moon ! the moon ! the moon ! How vast a power has the moon exerted on human life, physical and moral ! What wonder then at the lunar influence—take it in whichever sense you like—on the literature of all ages and peoples ! The moon has been the making of minstrels. Take away the moon, and not only is the volume of Poesy considerably reduced, but its character also is materially altered—into a thing stale, flat and unprofitable. All honour, therefore, to the moon !

The moon is a great remembrancer. All that

bards, ancient and modern, had sung of the Noor Jehan of the skies came rushing to my mind while maintaining my solitary watch on board at dead of night. Our Eastern writers are continually mooning about the moon and the lotus of the lake, but they never reach the chaste beauty, indeed the grand simplicity of the ancient European masters. It is a far cry from Homer to Kalidasa and from Kalidasa to Tennyson, but the lightning speed of thought embraces cycles and connects continents within the twinkling of an eye. The loyalty of literary subjection is above mere patriotic partialities, and even the "outer barbarian" of the distant East was involuntarily reminded of the grand old master Homer's famous moon-light piece which has employed the pens of so many English translators from Chapman and Sotheby, Pope and Elton, down to Derby and Dart, but which has not been better rendered than by the ever noble and now aristocratic Laureate. The following "experiment" falls short of perfection in only failing to reproduce the sweep of the grand Greek hexameters :—

As when in heaven the stars about the moon
Look beautiful, when all the winds are laid,
And every height comes out, and jutting peak
And valley, and the immeasurable heavens
Break open to their highest, and all the stars
Shine, and the Shepherd gladdens in his heart:
So many a fire between the ships and stream
Of Xanthus blazed before the towers of Troy,
A thousand on the plain ; and close by each
Sat fifty in the blaze of burning fire ;
And eating hoary grain and pulse the steeds
Stood by their cars, waiting the throned morn.

To linger in classic fields, my situation as the sole watcher of my camp afloat recalled that of Medea in the verse of Apollonius—the far from Colossus of Rhodes :—

Now rising shades a solemn scene display
O'er the wide earth, and o'er the etherial way ;
All night the sailor marks the northern team
And golden circlet of Orion's beam ;
A deep repose the weary watchman shares,
And the faint wanderer sleeps away his cares !

Even the fond maid, while yet all breathless lies
Her child of love, in slumber seals her eyes :
No sound of village-dog, no noise invades
The deathlike silence of the midnight shades ;
Alone Medea wakes ;

Or, to take a more familiar parallel, I was like unhappy Dido, in the fourth book of the Æneid, thus rendered by Pitt :—

'Twas night ; and weary with the toils of day,
In soft repose the whole creation lay,
The murmers of the groves and surges die
The stars roll solemn through the glowing sky ;
Wide o'er the fields a brooding silence reigns,
The flocks lie stretched beneath the flowery plains.
The furious savages that haunt the woods,
The painted birds, the fishes of the floods ;
All, all, beneath the general darkness, share
In sleep, a soft forgetfulness of care ;
All but the hopeless Queen, &c.

In fact, the classic Roman is conjectured, on tolerably good grounds, to have, speaking moderately, had his eye on the description of the degenerate Egypto-Greek epic. After all, there is nothing new under the sun, and it may be asserted that all the poets of antiquity drew their inspiration from their elders and chiefly from the eldest as "chiefest" of all, the Bard of the Iliad and the Odyssey—for the instinct of humanity sets its face against the Wolfian heresy. So the modern poets after them profitted by the labours of their predecessors. Perhaps the source of the night scenes of the great moderns, Shakespear and Milton, is to be traced to Virgil and proximately to Homer, the first painter in words of a night piece, unless the former be held to have been saved by his "little Latin and less Greek" from anything like conscious or unconscious imitation.

July 27, Sunday.—In the morning before daybreak, I heard from my bed Lakir and Kumud Babu repeatedly calling to the sailors to be up and doing. With some effort they were made to do so.

> The chain is loosed, the sails are spread,
> The living breath is fresh behind,

> As, with dews and sunrise fed,
> Comes the laughing morning wind ;—
> The sails are full, the boat makes head
> Against the Serchio's torrent fierce,
> Then flags with intermitting course,
> And hangs upon the wave,
> Which fervid from its mountain source
> Shallow, smooth, and strong, doth come.

We got out of the marsh and entered the river. There was not much of a breeze and such as there was was against us, so they poled and pulled on. We had a repetition of the usual process and the usual scenes. Our course lay mostly between sand-banks. We came upon many swamps, some of great dimensions, but none so extensive as the one we met with last evening. More than one went a good way near it in volume. Some we crossed. One or two seemed to promise us the same interest as yesterday, but after half an hour or so's sweep, we soon returned to plain water again. Plain, that is, by courtesy. Perhaps plain clear water as in the depth of regular streams, there is nowhere here. We had done with that yesterday. Either the greater part of our journey to-day lay through the deeper parts of marshes, where the aquatic plants abound, or the Teetas itself in these parts has the same mixed kind of liquid. The water throughout is interspersed with little patches of vegetation from plants shooting through it.

We have all along kept to the left bank of the river, that is to our right. *Towards*, I should properly say; for the bank—*terra firma*—is at a distance, for the most part at a considerable distance. Were the sand-banks on both sides all under water, this Teetas would be a worthy younger sister of its big brother the Megna.

THE END.

We have crossed our Ocean, at all events, though unknown, and are now in veritable *terra cognita.* Hitherto we have been drifting in the vasty riverine deep or floundering in the Dismal Swamp of the fen country—the dreary, dreary moor, now flooded and without end—ignorant of our position, not without an unpleasant uncertainty as to whether we were advancing or receding. We have repeatedly seemed to be the very argosy of the Poet's imagining,—with change of direction only :—

> A lonely ship upon a lonely sea,
> Sailing forlorn, upon forlornest quest
> To seize the secrets of the *East*,
> And wrench the bolted doors of worlds unknown—
> The due completion of the Zone.

It is over now.

> I now can see with better eyes,
> And *terrors of the deep* despise.

Our trial has ended. The vague and illimitable waters have been passed and we are on safe and familiar ground once more.

On this as on previous trips in the rainy season, to my mind the most interesting settlements on the banks are those narrow strips of habitation with water on both sides, indeed on all sides—each house an island. The people lead quite an aquatic life—the little imps playing to the very edge of the water, the older brats already trying their hand at fishing with rude little bamboo branches or twigs for rods, and the girls plying their little boats. To-day we saw very many hamlets and villages, sometimes single houses, round which the water has gone irregularly, filling up ponds and water-courses, drains and excavations of all kinds, and making little natural bays and creeks and minute harbours for the Lilliputian fleet of the rural population, the inner courts of houses being converted into wet docks, where the family can work upon the boats and load them and embark in them at ease from their house steps, secure from impertinent curiosity. This year it is not quite so good though as in other years when the God of waters is more lavish in his favours. I left bed rather late this morning, and learnt that we had passed Gokarna or Gopone, as it is vulgarly called. Natghur too had been passed. This was the seat of old Siv Narayan Chowdhry, one of the leading local squirarchy holding under, and owing allegiance to, the Maharaja of Tipperah, whose father or grand father had been the companion of his sovereign on his travels *incognito* in British India. Such connection rarely blesses, and the Chowdhry's declined until Siv Narayan was sold out of his lands. I had recommended his son Mohin to the Maharaja's kindness for a grant of his homestead and adjoining lands, which I believe he got. We enquired the name of a village and was told it was Sivnagar. I think I have heard another name associated with Sivnagar, by way of identification. It was a particular Sivnagar, for many are the Sivnagar s. For facility of recognition, the rule in India is to couple the name of a town or village cursed with a common or an an obscure name, with the name of a neighbouring town or village, usually the name of the best known or most important place in the vicinity. Thus we have Kheerpoy-Radhanagar, Polaberia-Jaynagar, Jamooa-Kandi, and so forth. The vegetation again attracted my notice. Here were a long series of the wild *Kool* (Bori as they call it, *Ziziphus Jujuba*), and the *Gambir* and the *Boroon.* One *Hijol* too I saw, the leaves eaten through by insects. There were some tall wild trees which we did not recognise, and for which the boatmen could give no names, some of them with beautiful foliage. One fine plant, Kumud Nath thought, was the Kántáli Chámpá. I plucked the fragrant leaves of another plant on the water's edge. The leaves look like those of the *Arhar*, but the plant is larger or rather more woody and strong, especially near the ground.

The next village is more important-looking from its houses. It *is* more important. We spy the sheds of a market place. It is not market day, but we notice some small bales of hill cotton stowed in a verandah. Some Mahomedans who are watching us give the name Maidagunj—a well known mart. There is a petty timber yard in which log cutting is going on. We enquire, whose is it? and some children mention some Mistri's (master-artizan's) name. We come upon a substantial-looking Hindu, evidently the mistri himself, directing his cutters at the brink of the water. Another timber-yard, and yet another! A little off from the boat's course, we see above a bend of the water, which goes right through the village away into the fields behind, a neat little square thatched room, belonging to a respectable villager, with a group of children standing in front. One is a rather young girl, apparently newly married, sporting her bridal or post-bridal robe. As Kumud Nath remarks, she has just returned in this *Sari* from her first visit to her husband's. That she is now in her father's house we conclude from the freedom she enjoys. She is better looking than the ordinary run of the sex among the rural population in these parts, and in her striped robe of bright scarlet she looks altogether pretty indeed. On our left extends a wide plain of paddy with patches of water between, and beyond is the distant skirt of trees marking the solid bank.

Yonder is the famous Dogangi marsh opposite Maidagunj, a fruitful source of litigation and loss to the landlords on the two banks for a long series of years. The standing *casus belli* I have, I hope, prevented for ever by my settlement of the disputed belt with the Sarail Zemindar on putni tenure in 1881, against the combined opposition of the officers and Amla of both sides. The late Jagunnath Bhattacharjea of Cossimbazar, Moorshedabad, venerable old gentleman, a Superintendent on the Sarail Estate, was the only man on that establishment who, faithful to his trust, seriously wished to end the perennial source of anxiety and waste. He was far advanced in years, yet it seemed as if he could not have rest, so long as this thorn in his master's side as it were, remained. So with his dying breath almost, he sought Agartala. His very superior in office looked with disfavour on the proposed negotiation. Perhaps he regarded the attempt to come to any arrangement with the Rajbari as a wild goose chase. And no wonder. Attempts had repeatedly been made and had all equally failed. The late Baboo Annada Prosad Roy Bahadoor, the proprietor of Sarail, then a mere boy, had himself come all the way from Moorshedabad to attend Maharaja Beer Chunder Manikya's coronation in the hope of conciliating the Durbar, but he found out his mistake at last, to say nothing of the many officers that he and his father before him had deputed from time to time to induce the Maharaja to come to an understanding.

Under the circumstances it was not strange if the manager of 1881 thought it would be a waste of time and money to keep one of his principal officers on such a hopeless mission.

After the usual compliments and mutual enquiries, and a good deal of other "chaff," the conversation naturally turned upon the subject of Dogāngi. We both lamented the bad blood which this little bone of contention caused between the principal Zemindar of Sarail and the Maharaja of Tipperah. The subject was then allowed to drop, but it came up again and again during the few days that Bhattacharjea remained at the Maharaja's capital. The old gentleman did not, of course, forget to advert to the origin of this possession of the Maharaja's. This was my weakest point. The river Teetas divides the two Parganas, Sarail, on the North, belonging to Roy Annanda Prasad Roy and the Dewan Sahebs, and Noornagar, on the South, belonging to the Maharaja. The swamp and sands of Dogangi are, however, on the

North bank of the river. Though thus geographically linked to Sarail, they formed part of Noornagar. Herein was the obvious source of conflict. The fact is, that the Teetas itself belongs to the Maharaja. Indeed, not to go behind the British period to times when all Trans-Megnatic Bengal belonged to the kingdom of Tipperah, the greater part of these Districts, if not the whole, including Sarail as well as the Sobhabazar Rajas' Gangamandal and the Bhookoylas Rajas' Patkiara, and other estates in British India, once formed an appanage of the Tipperah Raj. This is history, understandable of all, acknowledged by everybody. How Sarail became alienated from the kingdom, is a pretty romance of real life illustrative of the manners of our ancestors, well-known to all the inhabitants of the country to the East of the Megna who care about its past. The land abounded in forests—the haunts of wild elephants and of course the home of the leopard and the tiger. The people, almost *ex necessite*, were able sportsmen—their princes loved the chase of the nobler beasts to distraction. Once on a time, a Maharaja of Tipperah happened, in the course of hunting, by pure accident—a simple mistake—to kill the son of a Dewan Saheb of the day, who and his son were among his companions in sport. The remorse of the unwitting homicide may be imagined. It led him to give up the pleasures of the chase for the rest of his days. It might have proved hazardous to the unlucky perpetrator. In Mogul India, the death even by accident of a Mussulman at the hands of an unbeliever was usually paid for by the life of the killer or by his compulsory embracing of Islam. It was lucky for the Maharaja that he was all in all on his side of the Megna—a nominal allegiance and a share of the produce of the cultivated lands of the Megna valley being all that was paid to the masters of India by the least powerful of the Tipperah rulers, during the latter Mogul period. Vindictive prosecution being out of the question, even if the Dewan

Saheb had any mind to it, the afflicted father adopted a more respectable persecution. It was his only son that the man had lost at the hands of the Maharaja. The shock to a man of his years was so great as to unhinge his soul. The world lost all charms for him and he abandoned home and family and followed the Maharaja to his capital. The latter behaved right worthily. He too was minded to renounce the world and be a brother Durwesh with the poor Dewan Saheb. He was prevented from acting up to his inclination. Remaining in the world, he devoted himself to comfort the Mahomedan gentleman. After long patient endeavour, he succeeded. The disconsolate father was induced to return to the worship of his household gods and the enjoyment of his worldly goods. At last he returned home, dismissed from the capital with honor, and loaded with presents, not the least of which was Sarail. Thus the Dewan Sahebs became lords of Sarail. In time, it underwent division, until, in the progress of luxury and neglect among the owners, in default of the State demand, the lion's share (rather more than three-fourths) came to the hammer and was purchased by one of the ministerial agency in the District of Mymensing, Nursing Chunder Roy. Through his son Raj Krishna, and grandson Annada Prasad, the present Brahman minor of Cossimbazar has inherited.

And now to explain how the Dogangi Marsh, though topographically of Sarail, being on three sides bounded by it, came to be the Maharaja's even after the gift of the Pargana to the Dewan Saheb. The lord of Tipperah being the lord paramount of the country, and only Dogangi specifically being alienated, everything else, including the Teetas river bordering on Sarail on one side and Noornagar on the other, was left to him. I suppose the present Marsh was more of a lake in those days, forming a bay or gulf of the Teetas and remaining with it to the Maharaja. On the other hand, it is said by many that it was a former land-agent of the Maharaja's for Noornagar, who, by his activity and tact, aided by the judicious employment of money, during the revenue survey, got the Marsh pinned out, along with the river, within the boundary of the Maharaja's Estate. It must have been done on the sly, and was consequently unnoticed by the Sarail people. When, after learning that Dogangi had been included within Noornagar in the Survey, Baboo Raj Kissen Roy sued for it in the civil court, it was too late. At least the Sub-Judge dismissed the suit as barred by limitation. And so the matter was dropped, and ever since the Maharaja has claimed Dogangi. But though the case was not appealed or revived in any shape by the Sarailites, they did not give up their practical contention. They fought and bled for possession and spared no expense over it. Nor was there any lack of litigation, in consequence of the incidents of possession. And now the Sarail Superintendent, Jagannath

Bhattacharjea, reminded me of the origin of the dispute, and, urging that it was by an accident, even a *ruse*, that we had been enabled to lay any sort of claim to the property in dispute, appealed to our moral sense to wash our hands of it. The hereditary credit of this righteous Raj of Yudhister the Just should not be sullied by this trumpery temptation—this veritable *bagatelle*.

I could not offer him any hopes in that direction. However ready I may be, in a legitimate and moderate way, to advise, as a Hindu Minister of a Hindu Raj—indeed, a Bráhman Minister of a Kshattriya Raja—I was not prepared for such sentimental flights. Moreover, I knew they had no chance at the Durbar. The feeling on the subject of the Dogangi had been thoroughly embittered, while, apart from all question of feeling, a great many people of more or less influence on both sides were interested in keeping up the cause of dispute. The utmost I could hope to do was to settle the Marsh on business terms and end the eternal conflict and periodical drain. Bhattacharjea, of course, applied for the honor of introduction to the Maharaja Bahadoor, but I would not present him. He could not of his own right expect an interview, still less by right of his master. The principal would have been entitled to it as a matter of course, but not the agent. Besides, such consideration as might properly be due to an agent, poor Bhattacharjea was precluded from claiming by the informal character of his mission. He put his request on other and personal grounds. He was an old Brahman with one foot in the grave who had come from the far off sacred Bhagirati Valley, and sought permission to perform the ceremony of *Raj dursan.* He wished to acquire the religious merit which could be got by seeing a genuine ruling Kshattriya Raja. There is but one such sovereign left in Bengal, he pathetically added. I corrected him, saying that there were at least two. He shook his head gravely and answered that the other place was now, to all intents and purposes, British and the Raja was turned a Frank. At the same time, this fervid exponent of indigenous loyalty did not conceal—from me at least—a lower motive. It would give him additional respect at Sarail and on the Sarail service if he could see the Maharaja. I liked the old gentleman from the first, and these were ample reasons for my endeavouring to humour him, still I hesitated. The step seemed not without risk. I felt afraid of his springing a mine on us. Suppose he concluded his tender, as a Brahman, of blessings to His Highness, with a bold request, from his venerable Brahmanic self, for the gift of Dogangi to his Brahman master also of the Holy Land! The Maharaja would be in a fix: in the enthusiasm of piety of a moment, he might yield to the appeal. It was necessary to save His Highness from the horns, secular and sacred, of such a dilemma. Hence my caution. In justice to the stranger, it must be confessed that he had the taste and good sense not to attempt the Presence chamber by the back door, although he was familiar with the flunkies, at the house of one of whom I had provided him with quarters, who might have smuggled him into it. He moderated his ambition. Seeing that I had fathomed his motive, he frankly confessed his original programme, and abandoned his ecclesiastical diplomacy for a more secular work-a-day *role.* In fact, he threw himself on me. I said he must not hope for a free gift, and that I would oppose any proposition for conveying the lands by bill of sale. Nor was it necessary for his purpose, which might be served by a perpetual lease. This I could recommend, if he offered reasonable terms. After discussing these, he returned to Sarail, but not before I had sounded the Maharaja and procured his permission to tell the stranger that the thing might be done. Finding his colleagues indisposed, Jagannath wrote direct to Roy Annada Prosad at Cossimbazar.

The master recognising his interest, was not averse from a trial once more, in view of the improved prospect under my ministry in Tipperah. So, armed with instructions, Jagannath came to Agartala again. It was not difficult for me to induce the Maharaja, who had already expressed a favorable disposition. Other difficulties arose, however, almost as great as if His Highness were against any attempt at healing up the old sore. Obstacles from various sides and interests met the proposal at every step, and I feared I might have to resign, if only to prove my good faith. Otherwise, it might seem as if I had been beguiling the old gentleman into a fools' paradise, putting him to expense and trouble for nothing, and compromising him with his employer. Patience and prudence, however, ensured success. When Bhattacharjea had abandoned all hope, a settlement was effected, on terms very beneficial to the Raj. I received no credit of course, but was glad to save my honor and do a substantial good to the estate. There was little said about it afterwards by the Maharaja or at the Durbar, but, strange as it may seem, Baboo Annada Prosad felt so relieved at the successful issue of a thing he, after his father, had so long set his heart upon, that he formally thanked me in a letter full of cordiality.

We discern a steeple in the distance among the trees of the right bank. By the aid of glasses, we distinctly trace the outline of an old temple. It is the Sultanpore *mut.*

On and onwards we drive, poling up the Teetas. And now we spy the distant temple of Magra! Land, ho! Land! We are near the end of our tedious voyage, after all!

Still we have a good day's journey before us, at the present rate. Our sailors have been growing more and more sullen. They are evidently unhappy at the prospect. They feel that the thing cannot be staved off. For all their dilly dally and shilly shally, the evil day of their dismission—when their daily hire shall cease—is drawing at hand. Yet they will not give up their game easily, and they cannot command good grace at parting. They are by no means prepared to say

> Farewell! a word that must be and hath been—
> A sound that makes us linger—yet Farewell!

Masters of "masterly inactivity," they seem resolved on one last despairing effort in the Fabian strategy. They have not yet exhausted their excuses for tarrying on the way. At all events, they stick at nothing. Accordingly, they are continually leading us into the shallowest marshes. Every half-hour they wilfully stick the bark fast in the bed, and then proceed leisurely to draw it out of the hole. And then, having got it out, they would like to smoke to their success, before again sitting down to their oars or plying their propelling sticks. No wonder, we are going at a snail's pace, if going it may be called.

In three hours or so, we came upon the chief or about the only road of those parts, connecting the official centre of the Riding of—Brahmanbaria—the Sub-division as it is called—with the Head-Quarters of the County or District.—Comillah.

After a halt for breakfast at the ferry between the Sarail and Noornagar parts of the Brahmanbaria road, we proceeded on our journey. Having taken down the venetians, to ward off the midday heat and glare, we had escaped the important pastoral village of Bonguz. This is the stronghold of the milking tribe, being inhabited chiefly by Gopes. It is from here that Agartala draws most of its supplies of milk, so necessary to the sustenance of Hindu man and child and to the worship of Hindu Gods. The revenue had been farmed out, according to the old vicious system, to one of the court favorites, until I settled the village on the sub-talookdari basis on the leading milkman. I remember the place, too, as the port (so to speak) where, on a previous voyage, I put to, when my boat stuck in the mud and would not move, and where I for the first time beheld the spectacle of numerous boats being pulled through the bed of the river.

Getting up at 3 O'clock, after a quiet post-prandial nap, and looking out, while my companion still lay in bed, I observed the boatmen putting their vessel into an opening to the right. I was just in time to see the confluence of the Teetas and the Howrah, for such was it. The spot is desolate, without either human habitation or wild vegetation. Yet the prospect was not uninteresting, commanding as it did the bend of the Teetas some distance in the direction of Brahmanbaria station. The long curve of the Teetas is itself a thing of beauty, though unfortunately not a joy for ever, its charm being confined to the season, when the river is swelled by the rains and the tributes of innumerable rills and rivulets. Towards the end of the reach, lay before us—as we (for by this, my companion was up,) thought—Akhaora, though we recognised not Tilak Chakravarti's timber yard, (the only object we have heard of in connection with it,) or scarcely any village or dwelling-shed. It looked all desolate, like the rest. For the scene behind us was no more cheering. The very *mut* of Sultanpore, which was seen for long hours, was no more visible. By way of compensation, however, there was the steeple of Devagram peeping above the trees at some distance to the right of the mouth of the Howrah. This we now entered. We were struck by the tall robust jute plants, many of them 8 cubits in length, with which for the first time I saw the sands on both banks covered. The jute is new as a commercial article cultivated in the Howrah valley. Only within the last four years has the culture extended to this part. It has now run up to the very boundary of the Maharaja's State. Formerly, the Nalia (a corruption of our word Nailta) as the *kosta* or jute is here called among the agriculturists, was raised just enough for domestic consumption, for strings and ropes and for herbs for curries. Now the peasants know better, and cultivate for sale. Still the people up here hardly yet understand the full significance of the industry. The rates are still as low as before, ranging from twenty annas highest down to twelve or even lower, as I learnt at the Mugra office. I cannot help suspecting, nevertheless, that the middleman (Talookdar) extracts something more out of the jute lands. Higher up the Howrah, at Lohghar, where the Rajgi (Raja's territory) and the Moglan (British) meet—I was told by the husbandmen who followed my fleet, that the rate is even easier for this cultivation, being simply nominal—2 annas, or 3 annas only per biga—scarcely ever more than half a Rupee per acre. The reason given is that it is only the worst description of land, as they say, that is waste lands and sand banks, which will not grow rice, on which jute is grown. And land that will not grow rice is at a discount, that being the staple.

Although Mugra, the Head-Quarters of the

Maharaja's Agent for the fiscal circle *(Pargana)* of Noornagar, in the British district of Tipperah, and the *entrepôt* to the State, has been visible for sometime from the Teetas and might be soon reached from it by land, being, indeed, almost a stone's throw of the mouth of the Howrah, yet it took us nearly two mortal hours in coming up to it, the rivulet meanders in such a distracting mode. From last forenoon, we have been continually reminded of the neighbourhood of the Maharaja's territory by men in the passing boats or on the banks saluting us. As we advance, the tendency of the people is more and more to treat us as their own. The reception, though often rude enough, or even absurd, is artless and withal most cordial. There has evidently been a sensation in this part of the country at the news of the "advent." Here at least, on British ground, the people make no secret of their sentiments. Our appearance is hailed by all with lively gratification—by the oppressed poor as a relief. I would not be human if I was not gratified by this testimony to the faithfulness with which I discharged my duties and the zeal with which, under great difficulties, I tried to do justice to all. It were mere affectation in me not to understand it all. From the confluence, the welcome gathers intensity. More and more people meet us at every step and relate, some with tears, how from day to day they have been looking forward to our arrival. Ever since the announcement of the deputation to Calcutta, they have been speculating about it and since the receipt at the Maharaja's capital of the last telegram from Calcutta from the deputation, they have been in a pretty state of excitement.

They do not know, of course, that I am come for a short stay, on a limited mission, chiefly to give advice and depart. The higher classes too, though not equally demonstrative, are far from indifferent to our movements, hoping that at length the social difficulty—the war of castes —the "water question" as it is called—will be determined by independent and disinterested counsel and sympathetic treatment. It is the same in the Hills as in down-country. They tell us how anxiously I am expected at the capital and by the Durbar, how the city is glad, how the Amlah are speculating, how DHANANJAY Thakoor, the Chief Minister, looks forward to be helped out of his difficult and disagreeable situation in the Durbar, how the officers in general of the Raj reckon upon a "buffer" between them and the bullyism of the Residency, how the Maharaja has postponed everything to my arrival, how the intriguers and adventurers who have brought the State down to its present wretchedness, are in alarm.

The Deputy Collector on deputation for settlement work here, KALI KUMAR CHAKRAVARTI, and the Tehsildar, KALI PRASANNA GUPTA, came down to the fleet to see me; many others too came likewise. A select few were received in the drawing-room of the flag-boat. On the shore a great crowd assembled, the adults saluting from a distance and departing after a time, leaving the urchins to mount guard as it were, all through. There was no unseemly demonstration, no contortion of limbs, nor expenditure of lung-force. The display of animal spirits is voted vulgar, and before superiors even impertinent. All was strictly Oriental—grave, thoughtful, though with a cheery thoughtfulness. There are no voluble bards in Noornagar. and the howling Fakirs were at Agartala. And the simple villagers have not yet learnt the "address" trick. The reception, accordingly, was throughout pantomimic. There was no European hallooing—no hurry and bustle. The demonstration was marked by philosophical quiet and perfect ease. In the evening a palanquin was brought in and soon after dark I proceeded to the Mugra Rajbari which had been cleaned and illuminated for the occasion, where I held a kind of levée. I did not forget to make business inquiries about the place. I left the Revenue Office for the new office of settlement at which CHAKRAVARTI presides. I naturally felt somewhat interested in the office as of my creation and in the officers as of my own promotion. Then, KALI KUMAR is a grand master in the Fine Art of complimentary interpellation. Nay, not to be ashamed of giving any being his due, be he Cæsar or Satan, he is politeness itself, with a ready command of an eloquence that is insinuating if not convincing. He entreated me to accept of his hospitality. Although undisposed from temperament and habit to dining out and being, besides, in bad health for the moment, yet the request was made in terms which made refusal impossible. Like so many others, he solemnly declared that I had again come that way in very response to his prayers. He stopped not there, however, but added that *he* was *mine*. *I* had made him, maintained him in the State, advanced him in it, given him influence and means, rank and power. And all this from one who has been four times as many years in the service as I have—and one of the Maharaja's earlier favorites still enjoying a considerable place in His Highness's kindness, into the bargain! Again and again he protested that he owed everything of value to me, and he now begged of me the crowning favour—to ennoble him by thus publicly accepting of a few poor refreshments prepared by his family—in fact by his own dear Brahmani. He perfectly knew that my holiness as a noble Brahman from the banks of the divine Ganga (Bhagirati) is too pure and exalted for such a prayer, but then through all the Ages the Gods have been kind to their own devotees. Who could have the heart to disregard such an appeal, or turn his back on such a votary!

I give the speech in full as a picture of Eastern manners. It might possibly teach Anglo-Indian rowdies and civil and military scapegraces that there are at least natives and natives (to avoid the more offensive word,) and that we have a politeness and a chivalry of our own. For, it must not be supposed that there was anything degrading in this elaborate demonstration of deference, or the slightest alloy of a base motive in the proferred hospitality.

The house is beautifully situated in a distant corner of the artificial lake for which Mugra is famous. My host tried his utmost to make me comfortable, but his knowledge was not equal to his wishes, and, certainly, the resources at his command fell short of the requirements. He had, however, a high divan, beneath a broad punkah with a light narrow fringe, to seat me in, and my smoking engine and fireman with coke (prepared coals) besides a supply of musked sugared tobacco, accompanied me. Alas! the divan was not fresh and it was backed by a huge and lofty bolster, more suited, like an Elizabethan chair, for state than for lounging against, while the great horizontal fan overhead shook the bamboo beams by which it was held, creaking noisily at every pull and threatening destruction. Never mind! Life itself might be given up in return for the Vedic Hymn with which my host had waylaid me to his house. But there are nuisances not to be endured on any account, and such a one was the apparatus for diffusing light in that apartment. This formidable lamp of unglazed country earthenware, though kept in the corner, was a perpetual torture to the senses. I dodged about in various positions to avoid it, but the stench attacked me still. Finally, I gave up the struggle. As the dinner was ready only in a complimentary sense, if the cooking had yet begun, I begged to be allowed to retire on board, till called for. What a change from the stifling atmosphere of the house to the fresh air of the river! My host and everybody thought we must be miserable on board, but they have no idea of our vessel's roominess and its arrangements for comfort.

July 28th, Monday.—We were roused late at night—too late, indeed! But we asked no questions. It was useless to resist a Vedic Bard in the Kali Yug, and I let myself be conveyed over the dark and silent beach, to the place of sacrifice. We sat to dinner towards the end of the small hours, and by the time we returned to our dormitory on board, the grey streaks had insinuated themselves into the Eastern heavens. We soon roused the boatmen, huddled together as they were against one another, and sailed, or rather poled, up the stream. It was a wearisome, tantalising journey. The Nabinagar adventure over again! Mugra is fronted by some temples and backed by another. This latter one, belonging to the DAS family, was the landmark which long pursued us after the manner of the steeple near the junction of the Teetas and the Megna. The Howrah has a truly serpentine course. A few small cuts would reduce the distance to almost nothing.

A European missionary who had been up preaching in the Maharaja's territory, came down the stream and went past us. So new is preaching here, that the simple people said the Padre had been singing in the street.

Agartala at last! At 3 O'clock, we moor near my old Bungalow in New Town—Naya Haveli, as they call it.

Starting from Dacca in the afternoon of the 23rd July, without any halts of my commanding, I reach this capital in the afternoon of the 28th. It would take me the good part of another day in my lumbering craft to reach Old Agartala—Purana Haveli—where the Maharaja now mostly resides. Such, of course, is only the tediousness of travelling *en grand.* A man pressed for time might, in a small swift boat from Dacca, make a much quicker voyage.

AT AGARTALA:

GLIMPSES OF LIFE IN A HINDOO STATE.

As the fleet neared the close of its voyage, the number of the people who came to welcome my return and footed it all the way on both banks abreast of the vessels, became more and more, until the crowd, including many respectable men, was greatest at landing. Most of the officers and clerks and other gentlemen were, however, waiting at my Bungalow. The news of my arrival brought others, and a stream kept pouring in, until I retired late at night. It was so the next day; people were waiting in my house before my appearance. Thus the thing was kept up, from morn to noon, from noon to dewy eve, unto late night, for some days, by new men dropping in as well as by the same men coming again and again, from an idea of strengthening their interest or at least in the hope of creating influence with the people by a show of intimate connection with the—dog of the day. Fortunately for them, I could afford the leisure for the dissipation, before I saw the Ruler. The stars smiled on them; for the stars did not smile on me as they did not show a favorable time for the inaugural meeting with the Maharaja till some days after. At last, the prescribed day and hour came. I marched to the Maharaja's retreat at Old Agartala three miles off, across the river. Reaching the Presence, I pronounced my benediction and offered the complimentary gift of gold.

Since leaving Dacca, I had no educated company, and there was little prospect of any even at this capital from year's end to year's end. It was, therefore, with agreeable surprise that I beheld at my Bungalow the apparition of a respectable visitor from British India—

no less than the Joint-Inspector in charge of the education of the neighbouring British territory. Baboo DENONATH SEN brought with him and introduced his Deputy, Baboo BIDYADHUR DAS. They were travelling in the down country together, each in his boat, inspecting the schools, till they reached Mugra. From Mugra to Agartala is but a step, and so they poled up to this capital, if only for a peep into the Land of Lotos-eaters, the better to create self-satisfaction in their own activity. BIDYADHUR, who has been long in the Tipperah District, had, during my previous residence here, been well spoken of to me. DENONATH was an old acquintance. He is a man of mark in East Bengal, though I fear he has scarcely realised the promise of his earlier reputation. We first heard of him in Calcutta in 1875. It was the year of the Prince of Wales's visit. The British Indian Association having prepared a grand reception on the part of the native community, the Indian League, of which I had the honor to be the Chairman of the inaugural public meeting as well as the first President, proposed, at a great meeting on Christmas-day presided over by the Lieutenant-Governor, Sir RICHARD TEMPLE, to establish a permanent memorial of the royal advent. Anticipating by a decade the present cry for technical education, we purposed to found a great institution for imparting to the people instruction in the sciences and arts with special reference to their practical application to the conveniences and comforts, the wants and elegancies of life. It was in connection with the framing of a scheme that we first heard of the name of Baboo DENO NATH SEN. He was then head of the Dacca Normal School and was understood to have made certain improvements in the weaving-loom by which the famous cloths of that District were manufactured. Afterwards he gave up service to try his patent, but, according to the fate of all originators, he lost money by his enterprise, after all. Then he was invited to the management of Nawab ABDUL GUNNY and Son's estate, but after a short experience of the new Nawabate, he was glad to return to the fold of Government, in the Education Department. Latterly, he again wearied of schoolmastering or rather school inspection and took up charge of the Tipperah State, but he found the disadvantages and difficulties far more serious than those he had encountered in the Moslem's service. The Delhi comfit is difficult of digestion even by the seasoned stomach and SEN got sick at the first bite. In a few months he applied for permission to revert to his proper position in the Education Department of the Bengal Government in which he had earned his laurels and in which I hope higher honors await him.

In 1875 he was at the height of his fame, perhaps. His reputation in his part of the country was second to that of no man. And to us in the metropolis it came with all the charm of distance and the prestige of novelty.

Our Eastern friends spoke of him with enthusiasm. Men like the editor of the *Amrita Bazar Patrika* seemed to regard him as about the greatest East Bengali. At any rate, if Dewan KALI PROSUNNO GHOSE was the philosopher of Dacca, Head-master DENO NATH SEN was the great organiser with an original turn. Accordingly, we were pressed to invite him to our deliberations and ask him for a scheme. The pride of the metropolis would listen to no such thing. We thought we knew how to draw a scheme. But I prevailed upon my Calcutta friends to postpone their dignity for the national object. As we expected the bulk of our funds from the East—one gentleman from that quarter having actually subscribed Rs. 40,000—I pointed out the advantage of cooperation of a Dacca brother who commanded influence on that side of the country and who, with a distinct aptitude for industrial arts, was already in charge of a large educational institution. So the Baboo was communicated with. He expressed himself ready to come over, but he wanted the permission of the Director of Public Instruction. We mentioned the matter to Sir RICHARD TEMPLE and he passed the word to Mr. WOODROW, the Director. In due course, Mr. SEN came. The Calcutta Baboos naturally disliked all this ado for nothing, as they regarded it. For any lurking illwill that may have been harboured against the stranger, Baboo DENO NATH effectually disarmed Calcutta by his genuine modesty. His deportment was all that could be wished. It could not, though, obscure the unmistakable intelligence that beamed in his face.

At Agartala I was pleased to note that his shyness had worn off. In fact, from a staid, shrinking, taciturn man, he had become all forwardness and volubility. In the East, he doubtless felt himself at home, while the experience of so many years could not go for nothing on such an intelligence.

He brought with him a native practitioner

of Homœopathy employed at the Rajbari. A native of Jessore, he had long been at Dacca where DENONATH knew him intimately, so now the Joint-Inspector was come the Doctor came down from Old Town to see his friend. This Homœopathist's exterior is not prepossessing, looking as he does like a child of gaunt Famine, but he is favorably spoken of personally and professionally by those who know him. Of course, in keeping with the present deterioration of our society, he is deficient in manners; for a rather fashionable physician at an old capital like Dacca, singularly so. This was my first sight of him!

I offered my visitors *prosad* of course, but they were not sure of their arrangements and declined. The next day (the 12th) I found DENO Baboo still tarrying in the river, opposite the Political Agency, but he was still undecided, except that he must go up to see the Maharaja at Old Agartala or return to India forthwith. An unexceptional, indeed obvious, proposition, in the realisation whereof I could only wish him "God speed!" although, from my local knowledge, being not without my misgivings.

Thus armed with this unfailing alternative resolve, it was still not till the following day that he started in his boat—for the former. He was to breakfast on *Rajbhog*—ambrosial delicacies from the Rajbari—at his friend the Homœopathist's. But, as ill luck would have it, he did not reach Old Town till late in the evening! In consequence, he was detained there the next day. His movements already showed the Zone of the Lotos to which he had strayed.

THE CHRISTIAN VILLAGE IN TIPPERAH:

A Glance at the History of Portuguese Settlement in Bengal and of the Introduction of Artillery to the East.

During my first residence in Tipperah in 1877, I made an interesting "find." This was no less than the discovery of a Christian village in the heart of this frontier hill state. It is a suburb of the capital and bears the significant name of Mariamnagar. Indeed, situated between the Old Town and the New Town, it is, properly speaking, the native Christian quarter of Agartala. It is inhabited exclusively by Indo-Portuguese. Contemptuously ignored by the prevailing majority of the other races and creeds, they are scarcely noticed by new-comers, and, indeed, their physical, moral, and economical condition is so depressing and obscuring that a man might come and live here for a long time without being struck by an indigenous Christian neighbourhood. Genuine blacks all, without that variety of complexion among them which redeems the swarthiness of the other classes of the population and specially which protects the Aryan pretensions of Hindu and Mahomedan from rebuke, stunted in stature, without education of any kind, without instruction in religion, low in morals, addicted to drink and sexual vice, lost in spirit, poor and comfortless and despised, they give one the idea of Pariahs rather than Portuguese. Unless one keeps all his senses quite wide-awake, he is not likely to suspect any Christianish or *quasi*-European presence. But with ears on the *qui vive*, for anything curious or queer, he would not fail to be struck by the word *Feringi*—the Indian for *Frank*—which he might hear. The Frank here is the socalled Portuguese—in whom you discern very little European manners and still less European blood. VAN LINSCHOTEN, who came to India in 1583, was already struck by the degradation of his people in the East. At Goa, they "married freely with the ladies of the country," while the priests, by assimilating their views and ways to the superstitions of the natives, were enabled to make numerous converts.* In East Bengal, the conditions of their existence were too rough and precarious for the prospects of true matrimony with the women of the country—to say nothing of "ladies"—or for the progress of proselytism by persuasion. But the suasion of might still remained, and it was freely exercised. The outcasts of Hindu society could scarcely be compromised by any change. It was these that swelled the Portuguese community—from these that the European adventurers, specially the meaner Whites, found their brides. We have in the socalled Portuguese community of East Bengal at this day the descendants of that connection.

* Purchas's Collection of Voyages.

As found at Agartala, the Feringis are, I believe, the descendants of the Indian converts of the Catholic Church under Portuguese auspices—converted *en masse* by force rather than persuasion. They are a miserable-looking and truly miserable people, undistinguished from the rest of the masses, unless by a more sooty black colour and a lower stature, and perhaps a worse mental darkness. Marrying within their own body, they have, by the degeneracy of an originally low type, brought themselves to their present physical and moral degradation. For they are highly exclusive, and proud of their race and their faith, such as they are. Though visibly dying out, and feeling the want of suitable partners in marriage, they would not form connections with other classes, even if any were willing to join their community. In this way, they have preserved the purity of their primitive baseness—to indulge in a necessary Hibernicism in order to elucidate this absurd spirit of pariocracy.* They show no admixture with the non-Aryan elements of the neighbourhood—no Mongolian taint certainly; their features are Aryan. They look like the lower sort of Mussulmans, and are taken by many Hindus for such. But they hold the Mahomedans in contempt, and, were they not under a Hindu Government, might despise the Hindus too. They are Christians in their way, and are proud of it. They are proud likewise of their origin. Being uneducated, they have no history, but they cherish traditions of their former greatness. Doubtless, they still have, some of them

* I humbly submit for the acceptance of the learned this convenient term to express the aristocracy of the Pariahs—the nobility of the ignoble—the singular phenomenon of the pride of caste of the lowest castes. Sir John Phear's "bhadracracy" is also a useful addition to the Indian vocabulary, but it labours under the great disadvantage that the Bengali word *bhadra* itself is not understood by foreigners. "Pariah" is not only known by Anglo-Indians, but has long been a part of the English language.

at least, a modicum of old Lusitanian blood, however diluted with the poorest Indian—a Homœopathic dose, still potent for pride if for nothing else. For, the Portuguese merchants and corsairs who followed in the wake of GAMA to the East, could not have been attended by many representatives of the fair sex from the Iberian peninsula. Thus, though far from thorough-bred, or half-bred, though not Quadroons nor Octoroons, their claim stands to reason, in some measure. They are, if not Franks, a somewhat Frankish people. They constitute the *debris* of Portuguese Power ^ this side of India. They represent—but feebly, though—the adventurers who, in the sixteenth century, established formidable corsair states in the Bengali coasts and islands, and carried their ravages far and wide on land and water, thereby giving the great Mogul Empire its first serious shock from the outside by the sea.

The Portuguese settled in the second quarter of the sixteenth century in Bengal, where they established themselves in the neighbourhood of the ancient royal port of Satgong between the years 1537 and 1540. But their power in the Hoogly river was the brief blaze of a meteor: in 90 years all was over with it, their factory sacked and plundered, their stronghold blown away, its defenders killed in the storm, and the rest of the garrison made prisoners of war, the fairer of the fair sex absorbed in the imperial harem and the priests sent to Delhi—virtually as a curiosity of religion. Before that catastrophe which extinguished the Portuguese as a political factor in the Western channel of the Delta, they had become formidable on the Eastern channel and the Eastern and North-Eastern coasts. The country was divided between a number of independent rulers, of whom on the right bank the chief were the Rajas of Chunderdeep and Sripore. When in 1556 RALPH FITCH visited Bengal, the famous ISA KHAN, whose capital was situated some 20 miles to the South of Sonargong, had acquired paramountcy over all the neighbouring chieftains, and he was the Christians' friend. This traveller found the Portuguese settled in that part from almost the middle of the century, and in his time exercising considerable authority. The left or Eastern bank had, from time immemorial, been held by the king of Tipperah. The country along the Eastern coast had long been the bone of contention between Tipperah and Arracan. The Portuguese not only established themselves at the mouth of the Karnafoolee in Chittagong, but one of their sailors of fortune, SEBASTIAN GONZALES, seized the island of Sundeep and raised it to the doubtful dignity of a powerful pirate principality. The king of Arracan was himself a bit of a royal corsair, in his rude way, and doubtless felt an unfeigned respect for the desperate European adventurer as for a famous expert in his own line. Birds of a feather naturally flock together; here the *rapprochement* was accelerated by the Mug's experience of the stranger's might. Between them, these two friends—*Arcades ambo!*—ruled the entire littoral. Not content with this advantage, they penetrated to the interior, laying the country waste, massacring the inhabitants or carrying them away in captivity—the Christian sailor leaving the unbelieving Mug far behind in this diabolical distinction. This insolence and these excesses at length provoked the attention of the Government of India and the Viceroyalty of Bengal, and hastened the downfall of the evil powers. It was not an easy matter to crush the nuisance. The undertaking taxed all the resources of the richest satrapy of the Empire. The Mahomedan historians are silent as to the reason for the change of capital which at this time took place. But luckily the country had been opend to European trade and curiosity. TAVERNIER who, accompanied by the ingenious BERNIER, sailed down the Ganges soon after the transfer, says that the capital was removed from Rajmahal to Dacca in order to give protection to the Eastern parts of the kingdom, and the better to meet the Portuguese, who, encouraged by impunity, raided as far up as the banks of the Booriganga. Yet so difficult did SHAISTA KHAN find the task, that he resorted to low cunning and cowardly treachery, so unworthy of a true soldier or man. He divided the allied Portuguese and Arracanese, detaching the former from the latter by lure of better pay. Having employed the Portuguese in destroying the King of Arracan who had become a thorn and pest, he had his useful mercenaries destroyed when he no longer had any work for them.

The race was not, however, and could not be, exterminated. During their day, the Portuguese, specially the mixed breed, had largely multiplied, and formed many settlements in different parts. They did not soon forget their evil traditions. The danger from their depredations on sea to Indian vessels going out to the Bay, in the sixteenth century, may be still traced in Bengali literature in a curious verse, with an etymological interest, in MUKUNDRAM'S Argosy. Swept out of the sea, the remnants of the Portuguese—the survivors among the vikings and their descendants betook themselves to the humbler, but not the less disgraceful, *rôle* of river-pirates and marauders and robbers in general. They creeped into unfrequented creeks at the head of the Bay, or in secluded forests in the Sunderbuns or the neighbouring islands, whence they issued forth to cruise in the numerous waters of the Delta.

Their barks in sheltering cove below
Lurked for the passing peaceful prow,
Till the gay mariner's *sitár**
Was heard, and seen the evening star;
Then stealing with the muffled oar,
Far shaded by the wooded shore,
Rushed the night-prowlers on the prey
And turned to groans his roundelay!

**Sitár* is the Indian guitar. The Bengali mariner's instrument was rather the *bela* or *beala*—the Bengali violin. The word might be substituted but for its accent on the first syllable.

Thus the traffic in the lower part of the Delta was crushed, as the seaborne traffic had been before. Accordingly, their success at once necessitated and emboldened them to sail higher up, and far and wide, in search of prey. This continued down to a late period in the 18th century. Long after Portugal had ceased to have any connection with this part of India, when even Holland, her successor in the East, was herself struggling to keep up an appearance in Continental India, the rising British in Old Calcutta were wont to save themselves, as best they could, from a sudden surprise by these daring pirates, by the ludicrous primitive devise of a chain thrown across the river before the approach to their city from the sea! For the Indo-Portuguese did not confine their ravages on water, but led expeditions into villages and towns. Small parties committed dacoity and even burglary. Down to the earlier years of this century, the "black musty Feringees," as they were called, were the worst *badmashes*—

roughs, bullies and criminals—in the European towns of Bengal and their vicinity. The large lowland tract facing the sea, known as the Sunderbuns, was converted by them to its condition of a howling forest tenanted only by wild beasts and reptiles. Alas for poor Bengal, hemmed in between the Portuguese and Mahratta fires—attacked by land and by water—victim of marauders at home and of fillibusters from abroad! And what must have been the anxieties and insults and wrongs to which our ancestors were exposed during that anticlimax of our country's lot! And what gratitude do we not owe to the *régime* which has given us an exemption so necessary to peace and order.

Of the two, the foreigners were the worse enemy. The non-descript tag rag and bobtail equestrian rabble calling themselves Mahrattas, though composed of various Indian races and creeds, were bad enough, but they quickly relieved the people of their presence, leaving as fast as their worn-out country ponies could carry them with any little portable prize they could lay their hands upon. Their descent resembled the flight of locusts through the land. The people returned to their homes and resumed their cultivation or harvesting. The Portuguese, on the contrary, lingered in the waters of the Delta and, by scaring away population and industry, reduced a fine fertile tract to a wilderness not yet reclaimed during more than a century of strong government and civilised administration.

That constitutes a damning indictment against a European nation and their degenerate progeny. Yet, no picture can be all shade. And there is another side to the account of this miserable people. The credits may be few, but they are genuine assets.

Notwithstanding all that has been said, it was these old Portuguese who first introduced European arts and skill into India. Bengal in especial owes them thanks as well as execration. Our language has been enriched by them with a good many important terms. We owe to the Portuguese connection our words for *church*, *Christian minister*, *leavened bread*, &c. All our names of modern furniture are Portuguese. Throughout the East, the Portuguese have been the teachers of modern military science. For more than two full centuries, all the gunners in Asia were Portuguese.

In every sense, the first artillerists in the East—the earliest and greatest—were the Turks, whose naval triumphs had filled the world long before the rise of the maritime states of Western Europe. In Asia, the Turks naturally were the Gamaliels of military and naval engineering, at whose feet nations learnt—to whom armies were apprenticed. They were thorough artillerists—gunners as well as gun-makers. It was they or their Persian, Indian or other disciples, that constructed those grand old pieces of ordnance, at Agra as at Agartala, at Dacca as in the Deccan, which, long since pensioned off from active service, have become objects of popular worship, and which, exhibited as curiosities and relics of bygone prowess and civilization, still fill the beholder with astonishment. At any rate, it is matter of history that the grandest of them all, the *Malik-e-Maidan* or Lord of the Field of Bejapore, 14 feet 3 inches long and weighing 40 tons, was cast at Ahmednagar in 1548, by a Turk Mahomed bin Hassan *alias* Roomee Khan. He was a great engineer and true genius. The Todleben of his age, but without a White Tsar or black to secure his attachment with princely protection, he passed from service to service and from prince to prince, doubtless leaving in his track followers trained under him. In creeping round the remotest corner of the Old Hemisphere to start a through sea-connection for the exploitation of the barbaric East, the Portuguese laid their trust on their fire-arms. They had not only assured themselves of superiority, they had reckoned on a monopoly and even a miracle. Judge, then, their disappointment when they found the Indians at once provided and proficient! Conceive their mortification when, as sometimes happened, the Indian arms proved more powerful and precise and were better served than their own! Nevertheless, under the operation of the curse from which India suffers, the degeneracy all round which had set in embraced this head too. The old race of engineers died out and the people—their art forgotten and almost their knack lost—were ready to gape at the stranger's success as a marvel and glad to take lessons from him. From that time until the rise of the British, and the casting upon Asia of shoals of adventurers from the European Continent by the great French Revolution and the long wars, the Portuguese remained "master of the situation"—as instructor and gunner. A whole history is preserved in the etymology of a single word. In the early British wars, the queer term *Topaz* turns up again and again.

It meant artilleryman. But it was also a synonyme for Feringee—what would now be called Eurasian. And the Eurasian or Feringee of that day was commonly the Lusitanian or Indo-Lusitanian. *Topaz* in fact is *Topiwallah* or man of the *Topee*—the hat-wearer. The earliest hat-wearers in Indian waters were natives of Portugal.

It was in the same capacity that the forefathers of these Agartala Feringees came. Like other Indian powers, the Raja of Tipperah had his mercenaries. He had in pay Afghan infantry and Portuguese artillery. There have been difficulties with the Pathans, but the Portugese have always been loyal. The seat of Government was never long in the same place, and the Feringees carried their settlement along with the Court. Through all removals and vissicitudes, they have followed the fortunes of the Raja. And they are steadily dwindling with Raja and Raj. At Oodoypore, the old capital, they were a numerous and important community—now a poor hamlet holds them all and their entire insignificance. They are not even Topazes. Looking too like the Mahomedan peasantry of these parts, in shape and colour as in manners and clothing, they have not the distinction of even a head-dress to recall their European origin.

Almost by an accident, I discovered these "native Portugese" early in my first visit in 1876. I had not yet received my power. Invited to take up the management, I had seen the Maharaja and found him agreeable. There was no room for confidence, notwithstanding. Intrigue was unweariedly busy. Those who had victimised one minister—even to tarnishing his fair fame with the stigma of corruption—might well hope to keep out another. I repeatedly asked permission to return, but the good Maharaja detained me from day to day with promises of an early settlement. It was the height of the rains, and there was then not a metalled road ; besides, prudence confined me to the quarters assigned me. I utilised this period of suspense in acquainting myself with the country. My purpose was facilitated by the numbers of men of all classes that visited me or crowded round my house to have a sight of the great new-comer. Inquiring about the supply of liquor, I learnt that the Tipperahs produced it themselves at home by fermenting boiled rice, but that the best kind was made by the Feringees. Feringees? What! were there Feringees here too? I exclaimed, and called for some of them. Thus they came, a wretched half-dozen, of whom only one JOAKIM was worth conversing with. It was lucky perhaps that they were thus brought to my notice. For they were on the point of leaving Agartala "for good." Their fortunes were at the lowest ebb. They had been reduced by death and distress from a thriving community to a few struggling families. Their occupation as gunners had long since gone, for Tipperah had long ceased to be a fighting power. Beyond a few old pieces, without proper equipment, there was hardly any artillery to speak of. Still they occupied an honorable position in the military service. But latterly they had been elbowed out by Hindustanis, Tipperahs, Muniporees, and last not least by Gorkhas. The Bengalis of low type in Court had no sympathy with a people neither Hindu nor Mahomedan. They found it difficult to maintain themselves, to say nothing of keeping up their Christian position. And now they were crippled in the means of continuing their race. Their own little village no longer afforded a sufficiency of brides for them. They had so far gone down that their brethren in British India would not form connections with them. They were being invited for some years by their relations in Noakhali to come and settle among them, with offers of lands and other assistance. They had at last decided to go. I thought them too valuable an element in the population for the state to part with them. I advised them to remain, promising, when I was appointed, to attend to their grievances and try to make them somewhat more comfortable. Accordingly, when the opportunity came, I made good my word, as much as possible. I introduced the able-bodied who offered themselves into the military, and maintained them in it almost in spite of the Agency with its exclusive regard for Goorkhas, and gave JOAKIM rank.

The Feringees are at any rate not an ungrateful people. For when next the pastor, who is annually sent by the Church to minister to their spiritual wants, came, they mentioned to him all that I had done or tried for them. Accordingly the reverend Father one day held a mass for my benefit.

This will explain the following entry in my diary of the present visit.

12th September, Friday.—I was visited by Father JUSTIN CLERICI, O. S. B., the Roman Catholic priest of Noakhali, who has come for ministration at Mariamnagar. He is an Italian from the Genoa district who had formerly been in Africa, in Tunis, which he left just before the war. He went to England before he came out to India, where he is now two years. First posted to the Feringee settlement in Bikrampore, he is at present in ecclesiastical charge of the Indo-Portuguese Catholics of Noakhali, where there is a brick-built church and parsonage.

He does not speak English fluently or idiomatically and expressed great surprise at my proficiency. I must have been in England, he thought. The old story! So his Bishop of Dacca and the Rev. Mr. ALLEN, the Baptist Missionary of the same city, said on board the steamer from Naraingunge, when last I was going home from Tipperah in 1881. So Major SMYTHE in the train from Calcutta on my first journey to the far East. So General SHOWERS at Moorshedabad so long ago as 1864, and fifty others, at different times. Devoting ourselves as we do to the language and literature of our rulers, it is agreeable to know that our efforts do not all go for nothing. For the rest, it was their ignorance of native society that disposed these good gentlemen to regard me as a prodigy of linguistic attainments. There are as good fish in the sea as out of it—as good scholars among those who have remained all along within the limits of India's "coral strand" as among those who have ploughed the sounding main. That, much more than the existence in our midst of a handful of men who have returned from Europe, is a significant social fact, and, I may add, an important political factor.

I may here note that in the steamer in question, the two ecclesiastics had hot and interminable controversies, and both constantly referred their polemical differences to me, complimenting me on my theological knowledge. In the ardour for victory, each protested —this rather confidentially to me—that I knew more of the Bible than the other. If there were other Europeans on board, they were too ungodly. Both the Catholic Church and the Baptist Chapel on board assured me that I more had hope of salvation than the among our scoffers fellow-passengers. Amen!

Father CLERICI was even more surprised to find me talking glibly on Italian affairs, about NAPOLEON III, CAVOUR, GARIBALDI and RICASOLI. The NAPOLEONS he of course claimed as Italians. My sympathy for Italian unity, however, did not receive any response from him. He was entirely a Catholic. He was dead against VICTOR EMMANUEL and bewailed the loss of Rome to the Church and the confiscation of the Temporalty. He was bitter against the seizure of the Estates. Compensation in annual payments was offered but refused by the Pope, hence the missions are in want.

He complained to me as the Temporal Power against a DOMINGO MERCER, Feringee of Mariamnagar, who having committed adultery with a woman from Sylhet, now refused to marry her. Foriadan is his real name. He is 26 years of age, and he eloped with her from the Feringee community of Bondasil in the east of Sylhet. I summoned all the elders to attend and between them and myself persuaded the young man to take her to wife.

It was during the rainy season that I went. Indeed, at any other time of the year I could not make a through voyage. There would not be water enough for any but the tiniest craft, and even these would have to be pulled through the bed by sheer force—and sailing up the Howrah in my budgrow to Agartala would be out of the question. But the rains this year had been scanty. It was proportionately hotter than usual, and day and night one had either to plant himself under the *punka* or to cause the great palm fan to be waved in the neighbourhood of one's person. At length, the long deferred rains entered appearance. On the 30th August there was a slight preliminary sprinkling. But there were signs in the heavens that the monsoon had burst in Bengal, in the districts washed by the Bay. September opened with clouds and a drizzle. There was no more shying or shamming. The following day the floody Jove turned the screw of his tap and opened his streams on us. And so it went on, from day to day, for days together, raining cats and dogs. At first a relief to all, it gradually proved too much of a good thing ; not knowing to stop even there, it finally degenerated into a nuisance. The very husbandmen, who had been before complaining in despair of Nature's niggardliness, and afterwards loudly blessed Heaven as they wallowed in the mire so necessary to the life and growth of their insipid rice plant, the very husbandmen cried *Bus!* Enough! More than enough! For God's sake, stop! The god of the weather listened. He took them at their word. The rains stopped with a vengeance. Then the drying process began. Alas! we were never to know the *juste milieu.* The golden mean was a dream of the Golden Age. All the moisture was screwed out of us all, earth and air, man and beast. We gasped for breath. We cried like so many weak saints under *auto da fé.* Nor was this the worst of it. In the last week of the month an epidemic arose. The Cholera decimated our ranks. Appearing first among some coolies in the bazaar, it spread, and soon entered the palace. First a servant died, then one of the Heir Presumptive's (Bara Thakur's) *kachooas*—concubines—and another. The matter looked serious. A consternation seized the Rajbari. The Maharaja fled with his immediate family to New Town—the capital proper. It was a most inconvenient time for such changes, on the eve of the Doorga Pooja. We were already in the midst of the introductory festival when the outbreak commenced. It was difficult to transport and accommodate all the persons and chattels, for the harem is a host in itself. But the situation was urgent, and despotism is capable of revolutionary vigor. Orders were simultaneously given to collect, on the one hand, boats and palki bearers, and, on the other, to put the old apartments in New Town into tolerable repair. Before they were fully executed the move had begun. They were expected here on the 26th September, the opening day of the Doorga Pooja Proper. In reality, the Maharaja and family arrived the next day, the Great Eighth of the Moon, as it is called, or the second day, held peculiarly sacred. Before that the whole place had been deserted by the movable part of the population. All the trades and nearly all the offices are filled by out-siders from British territory. A consternation seized them and they fled. An epidemic of a deadly disease is everywhere a serious matter. Here the quarrantine that is observed on such occasions, rude and mild as it is, is looked upon with far greater horror. There is better treatment available here, doubtless, than in the villages in Rural Bengal from which most of the residents come. But the Bengali more than any other loves to be with his family, and certainly prefers to die among his own people in his native home than in Paradise itself. Hence the haste to get away; the local difficulties of those post-mortuary rites, without assurance in respect of which no Indian in prospect of death can be happy, strengthening the motive for flight. As they passed my gate, they wondered what I should still be tarrying for in this land of plague, beyond the strict limits of the Hindoo Pale. In their anxiety for safety, they frequently forgot the usual courtesies. Those who caught the eye of any of the superior members of my establishment just looked in for a moment. Others, however, even in their run for life, stopped to secure the good offices of the great Brahman at such an hour of trial, while many another, with calm prudence, by a momentary halt at my house, in the midst of that retreat of panic, provided for the interests of Number One, in case both sides might be spared. They all came with their parting respects for their parting blessings. They did not leave without loudly expressing their concern for me, and advised and begged and prayed me to depart. Their counsel was the more rational that there would be no business during the vacation, in consequence of the Festival, with or without the Cholera. But I was in no mood for moving, except to go home for good. Besides, nothing could be done without taking leave of the Maharaja, and there was no getting at him during the panic. One gentleman, a landlord of the Bikrampore Riding of Dacca importunately pressed me to leave Agartala and live on board boats in some of the great rivers in down-country till the health of the place was restored. I had been fairly tired of boating, still cruising in the Megna might have been a temptation in the face of a miserable death, but there were practical difficulties. No boats roomy and convenient were to be had, and by the time they might be ordered up from Dacca, the question of life and death would have been settled. Either I would have turned to ashes or the epidemic would have passed away, leaving me intact. So I maintained my character of fixture, remaining where I was, trusting on God. And I was glad to find my people of the same tranquil philosophy. For, in case a genuine anxiety for life had seized them they would have been sure to desert, with or without notice. We were the only party, of all who were free to go away, who stayed. It was a dismal prospect, with the whole country around weeping and wailing, to be cooped up in our corner, confined to our quarters, without intercourse with the world, the exposed pauper dead, dragged like dead dogs past my house, being about the only human figures I saw. However, we managed to get on and even to keep up our spirits, without which, indeed, we should certainly have fallen victims to the dire disease. At one time there seemed cause for alarm. One of my people was attacked one morning with purging. So General Cholera had invaded my camp and penetrated into it! My servants were terrified. I had a whole colony of Ooriyas who looked the picture of anxiety and were doubtless ready to flee. Luckily, it proved a case of diarrhœa. The man soon recovered. We had no other domestic complaint or difficulty.

My house is out of town as it were, in what may be called the European part of the town, although just now only one European or East Indian lives here in the person of the doctor who is head of the medical department. It is a lonely enough locality in the best of times, and now not a mouse stirs. The only beings I ever see are two neighbours, a medical adventurer from the North, a jack of all systems, who has just set up here as a native doctor, and a celebrated musician, Kasem Ali by name, descendant of the historic TAN SEN of AKBAR'S Court. They had seen many places in India, each in a different direction, and from their intelligence they might be valuable acquaintances if one could be sure of his ground. They balance one another, acting as mutual foils, if not as correctives quite. The Mussulmans of Lucknow, from which KASEM ALI comes—*viâ* the King of Oudh's Colony, Calcutta—are famous for "tall talk," and KASEM ALI Khan avails himself to the full of his birth-right, but for drawing the long bow, this adopted son of Æsculapius from Mymensing will be a match for all the Mahomedan musicians any day. Between the two, I managed to get on pretty lively.

At times nature would rebel. Thus I find my entry 'What a horrible confinement is this! I am literally cooped in my bungalow.' And so on.

On the second of the Festival, I ventured out towards the close of the day as far as the bend of the street and river and took my seat on the public way in front of KASEM ALI Khan's house. He was gone out to pay his respects to the Maharaja, but his woman of a wife (as he has latterly made her, who had been a public singer and, of course, of the *demi monde,*) was good enough to send out chairs and stools for me and my companions, (KUMAD NATH and the doctor,) with spices and odours. The famous dilapidated tin-box, country-made, (and oh how wonderfully!) containing, by hook or by crook, a great quantity of valuable otto of sorts, was laid bare before me, with a candle light placed beside, for us to help ourselves.

I did not stay long there. After my return KASEM ALI Khan came home and followed me. The mystery of the odoriferous Moslem was revealed by him this day. Mahammad (God bless his soul!) loved sweet scents, flowers, amber and musk, *utturs* and perfumed oils. The Koran recommends perfumes and flowers to the Faithful. A merchant from Aleppo used to visit the Prophet every year, bringing sweet scents for him, and fruit for his grand-children. Tailoring was then in its infancy; at any rate, pockets had not been invented, sleeves doing their duty. The children used to put their nimble little hands into the traveller's capacious sleeves, stuffed with various delicacies. On one occasion the Angel Gabriel appearing to Mahammad in the guise of the Aleppo merchant with a Sura of the Koran from the Almighty, little Hasan and Hossein as usual ran up to him as to their familiar friend. The Angel took them on his lap. They, as was their wont, searched his sleeves. The Angel inquired of the Prophet what they meant. When it was explained, Gabriel immediately brought down (without leaving his seat) apples, pomegrantes and grapes from Heaven, and offered them to the dear children.

The precept of the Koran and the example of the Prophet recommend as well sweet-meats as sweet scents. Hence the addiction of the Faithful to both. Mahammad loved roses to distraction. When a beautiful Bussorah was given him, he smelt it and placed it in his eyes and his forehead. Hence the religious veneration in which the rose is held, in especial. No good Mussulman will tread on flowers. None will take the rose to his bed even.

20th September.—They are all leaving us! It is particularly galling for the home-loving Bengali to stay abroad during the Great Doorga Pooja. And here this year the approach of the Cholera is an additional motive for clearing out of the place as fast as one can. My only neighbours—of the Agency, next door—too are going. Since yesterday the Baboo's boat is at anchor. This morning a message came to me for permission to my chairmen to palanquin the

Beebee* over to it. Some time after, Baboo UMAKANTA DAS himself called, to take leave for home during the Vacation.

Thus this family escaped the Cholera season. But they exchanged one evil for another. They passed a miserable Doorga Pooja at their Pubna home at Teota—seat of Raja SHAMA SHUNKER ROY, who and his brother PARVATI were associated with me on the Indian League, as among its chief supporters. They all fell ill, as they always do, whenever they go home. Their country seems to be infested with fever. They were glad to get away as soon as they could move, consistently with the health of some of the party.

The first day that I visited him here I found him in a great state of excitement. He sat up in his bed as soon as he saw me enter and insisted on shaking hands with me. His hand

* I consider "Beebee" the true *feminine* of "Baboo," and I hope it may be so used by others as a substitute for "Mrs." or at least by way of a variety.

was hot. He conversed with more than his wonted volubility and rapidity of utterance, whether I spoke or no, coming down on me with a harangue for a simple inquiry about his health. He was not himself, poor soul! It was all his native fever—bred of malaria in the swamps of Pubna. Next day, I found him easier, and he said he was all right. The third day, however, there was a relapse. He again got well, this time without mistake, he hoped. For he had had no fever for two consecutive days and nights, and looked almost hale and uncommonly hearty. Neverthcless it were prudent not to exult too soon. This disease is a mischievous imp that seems to delight in playing at hide and seek with its victims. I better proceed with my diary.

17th October.—As I feared Baboo UMAKANTA'S fever had assumed a quotidian type and the paroxysm might return today, I became anxious, specially as the poor man is suffering with his whole family, his house being turned into a hospital. So I sent my Jamadar AODAN SINGH at noon to inquire and was relieved to know he was yet well. In the evening as usual I visited him myself. Found his physician in attendance. The Baboo welcomed me smilingly, saying he was sitting up in bed. I hoped I might never again see him stretched at full length, moaning from ague. As I approached the cot, KASEM ALI Khan, who was sitting beside the patient, got up in my honor and saluted me in style, a courtesy which I returned to the full, while Baboo UMAKANT introduced to me Dr. * * * * *, who rose to meet my proffered hand. I then took my seat, followed by the Doctor, but KASEM ALI Khan still remained standing, as in the Vizier's presence, notwithstanding Baboo DAS'S request to him to sit down, till formally asked by me to take his seat. Of course he preceded the operation with a profound and elaborate salaam. I immediately began to make inquires of the patient about himself. But the polite Mussulman had not yet done with me. As soon as he got an opportunity, bending over with joined hands, he inquired of my Huzoorship's Temper. I suitably acknowledged his politeness with a grand "Al-ham d ul'Allah! God bless you!" which must have amazed the unsophisticated Doctor and the Political Baboo.

We had then a desultory conversation, among other subjects, on medicine. On that we received no particular light from our professional partner. I was, however, glad to find the Doctor no very heroic practitioner. He had prescribed for Baboo DAS half grain doses of quinine. About the action of the drug he was quite at sea. Nor did he leave any impression of general attainments. For science in general out of the region of the healing art he expressed supreme contempt. Spectrum analysis he had not heard of, as he did not correct me, nor seemed to see the mistake when in the hurry of delivery I once called it "spectroscopic analysis"! But he cared not for it, whatever it might be, saying, what was the good of all these things? He had been in many districts of Bengal and even in the Bay and to the Malayan islands. He had surveyed the Andamans preparatory to its being utilised as a convict settlement and had been twice shipwrecked.

He left me with the Baboo, and thereafter KASEM ALI Khan too went away, for his prayers as Mr. DAS thought, but really to give us an opportunity for any confidential conference we might want. In return for so much politeness and thoughtfulness, I looked in at his house before returning home, sitting with him for two hours or so.

19th October.—Vakil NOBOKUMAR SEN, late State Advocate, visited me on return from a trip to Noornagar to look after a Talook which, he reminded me, I had given him (while making the settlement of the Pargana) and in respect of which I had relieved him (in due course of business) of certain arrears of rent. Of course he saw his friends down country. One and all, rich and poor high and low, inquired, whether I had been invested with the ministry with full authority, saying they were on tiptoe of expectation and ready to burst out in joy. As soon as they heard of the commencement of my administration they would call to present their respects.

SEN related his sufferings on the trip. He complained of the new mosquito plague. Mosquitoes were never rare birds in the country, but they have multiplied to an inconcievable and intolerable extent. The air is filled with the stink of jute—it was impossible to breathe —not a square inch of pure air is to be had in the whole country. How the people managed to live, he wondered, said he. It was worse than dung—the jute decomposition. Worse than the vilest animal excreta! he exclaimed. My own language! thought I, as I remembered my experience on a Doorga

Pooja evening at Jonye, when walking from the boat to the mansion of the MOOKERJEES, I was obliged to run for life from the stench.

SEN got no fish to eat and had to live on pulse, which is the detestation of the Eastern Bengali who, by the way, don't know how to cook it. The minute fry which nobody except paupers touched, was welcome to the table of the richest. There is no fish, in consequence of the state of the water from jute decomposition. I wonder whether Government ever heard of this fish famine. What is Mr. DAY—the salaried fishmonger about? Here is a bad prospect for fishy Bengal.

21st October.—I assist my Ooriahs in filling up their P. O. forms for remittance :—

Zilla Balasore, P. O. Dhamnagar, Police Outpost Roipur, Pargana Káimá, Mouza Moá, Remitter—Náth Dás, to Hádibandhu Poira, Rs. 10. Also Rs. 18 to Lakhan Bearer in Mouza Bhuipur, in the same Zilla &c., from Punand Bearer, Agartala, remitter.

Again Rs. 10 to Bonamali Palái, Mouza Pahná, same Zilla, &c., from Dám Palai, Agartala. The other day I wrote for one Oorya servant, and KUMAD NATH, I believe, wrote for another. One other then remains to send thus his rent.

With the exception of one who belongs to Patámoondi, (formerly belonging to the Baboos of Taki and Baranagore, then of the SINGHS of Calcutta, now the estate of the late Raja DEGUMBER MITTER, C. I. E.,) all my Ooryas are tenants of Baboo NIMAI CHARAN BOSE, Roy Bahadoor, of the family of the great millionaire KRISTO BOSE.

Went to the Rajbari, New Town. Sat in Bara Thakur's room seeing books and photos. The most interesting of the latter were portraits of the Maharaja from negatives taken some ten years back by a French artist who gave himself the classic name of Apollonius or Apollonais (or was it the whole hog, Appelles ?) —the same whom the present Mrs. * * * * had accompanied as wife, though she now flies in the face of the suggestion, protesting she never had been in Tipperah or, for that matter, in East Bengal at all! As if the Maharaja's artist's eye could make a mistake in identity of that kind! They are all good likenesses of the Maharaja at his best, representing a noble-looking Aryan Prince that he is—a good specimen of a Bengali gentleman—in youthful health and freshness, without anything of the worn-out aging expression which is invading his countenance of late years.

The Bara Thakur made me a desirable present of some two dozen unmounted photos, copies of larger photos and pictures from Europe, as well as prints from original negatives in his possession, consisting of ethnic studies and scenes in Tipperah. His own photo formerly taken by APOLLONAIS does not at all remind one of him. Not only is the complexion darker in the picture but the features seem somebody else's.

I ought to note that as soon the Bara Thakur saw me he enquired of JOGESH and SATIS whom he had seen at Calcutta, before I could convey their *pronam*. He has seen the newspaper notice of poor NORESH'S death, and spoke of it with feeling. He was also good enough to say he had read with pleasure and profit the account of my Trip from Calcutta to Dacca published anonymously in the papers.

I was then called up to the Presence. Footing up a long broad flight of rather deep stairs, straight after the first few steps, to the upper storey, I passed through a room filled with valuable goods in glass-ware, cabinet-ware, ivory-work, gold and silver plate, with musical instruments, scientific instruments, &c. I was next ushered into a large and airy verandahed room furnished, indeed only less crowded with furniture,—towards the centre a charming ivory chair beside an indifferent mahogany table surmounted by a costly clock under an old fashioned chandelier,—here a neglected piano, there a brand new first class microscope,—rich carpets and hangings heaped up in a corner, a silver half-drum *(bayan)* and a full-drum *(pakhawaj)* mounted with ivory balls, in another,—guns in boxes and guns without, swords naked and sheathed, shields and spears of sorts, paint boxes, stereoscopes, opera-glasses, leather bags and carpet bags in profusion,—telescopes leaning against walls or lying about on the floor,—and what not besides,—on a side whereof I found His Highness seated on the Indian bed of comfort and state called *gadi*—a roomy mattress stuffed thick with cotton-wool—backed by an enormous round bolster and flanked by diminutive flat pillows. After the preliminary mutual greetings, as soon as I had taken by permission my seat on the rich Persian carpet specially placed for me, His Highness first enquired of my health and then mentioned the illness in his house...

Last Sunday being Dewali or Kali Puja, they

expected me to illuminate my Bungalow as on previous occasions when I stayed here. As I am a loyal conformist, even to paying the periodical Bukshish to the Rajbari servants, I thought I should not decline the obligation of lighting up my premises. I gave my people orders accordingly, and to do the thing on as great a scale as before, with if possible still better taste. Thus my place was grandly illuminated, with better effect than the Rajbari lighting—which is nobody's business. The only check on neglect and *loot* there—that of the master's eye—was absent. The Rajbari servants doubtless knew that it would be so: at any rate, they could make it so, without rousing the suspicion of their masters of playing into menial hands. His Highness never comes out, and this time even the Princes did not stir out. Nay, my neighbour-friend KASEM ALI Khan, who usually comes this way, did not step out—why, I wonder. Is it because he did not light up his house? I took a walk in the evening to go round my grounds and go out to the streets to see. In passing Khan's place, I met him sitting with SULLOO, once a professional athlete now a travelling shawl seller, in his verandah. He seemed to be morose, or he would certainly have joined us.

On this visit I observe a change in domestic and commercial architecture in the East—namely, the use of corrugated iron in roofing. It has penetrated to these hills even. In 1881 I caused some dissatisfaction by my order for covering the grass or reed thatching of the shops at Agartala with a thick matting of bamboo splinters. My object was obvious—to minimise the number and extent of the fires that occur in a land of combustible bamboo and grass houses, specially during the dry months, reducing all personal property to an uncertain possession, and making life miserable from anxiety from day to day and from hour to hour. I hoped at least to prevent a general conflagration from the living cinders of straw or burning grass and bamboo ch'ps wafted by the air to other houses. Yet the leading tradesman (SRINIBAS Shaoo of Dacca) alone readily and cheerfully submitted to my proclamation. Within these three years they have all progressed in civilisation beyond my immediate expectation. The nearest approach to iron roofing that I remember having seen in 1881, was in a private house in the Manipooree quarter, where an ingenious man had given the thatch of his hut for his god a tinned plate covering by collecting a number of apparently rejected empty tin cases and piecing together cuttings from them! This time I saw at Mugra two new rooms belonging to RAM SUNDAR BHUIA of this city (managing partner of the shop known as Hole Sen Company, corruption I fancy of Wholesale Company) with spelter roofs. Here too I observe several shops adopting the same. I hear that at Comillah, Mymensing and other cities all the shops have got this roofing—no other is allowed by Magistrate or Municipality. It is being introduced into the country at large too, as distinguished from the country towns—not in vanity but purely as a protection from fire. The commencement of this improvement dates not beyond the last four or five years. It has become general within the last two years. I am glad to think that I paved the way for it in this State.

7th November 1884, Friday.—We were talking of the health of the season. All three, KUMAD NATH, the Doctor RAM CHUNDRA, and myself, complained of headache. The doctor attributed it to the atmosphere, adding that it made people occasionally feverish. I certainly feel this slight feverishness at times. He complained of the water here, saying that, with the exception of the Agency pond, there is no good water to be had anywhere. Other artificial waters may look clear, but on bathing you immediately get aching at the back of your head. It is all nonsense, the outcome of ignorance and the Bengali prejudice against hills !

This, to be sure, is a time of year particularly unfavorable to health. The season is bad everywhere in Bengal. Some parts of the country become particularly dangerous. In Dinajpur and Rungpur, there are fever cases in profusion. It is, said the doctor, a bad type of fever, commencing with typhoid symptoms, soon developing convulsions and in 3 or 4 days making an end of life. In Mymensing it is nothing at all like that, though there is bad health generally and many cases of fever occur, as in other districts.

CURIOUS CUSTOMS.

[*My Diary at Agartala continued, under date the 7th November, 1884.*]

AS in other countries so in this, there are popular practices peculiar to the several seasons. I heard of a curious custom of the border districts of the North. The people make a human effigy of straw, large as life, and stick a long bamboo in its back. This image they set up on the last day of the month of Kartik and carry it about with beat of drum and fanned with winnowing fans, until they dismiss it with many indignities, as the Evil Genius of the Season evidently—with this address—*Come Good! Begone, you Ill! And death to mosquitoes and flies!*

It is true that this is the time of mosquitoes, flies and insects of all kinds, which are a great nuisance at night specially. With the close of the Indian month of Kartik, corresponding roundly with October, their strength is reduced to a minimum. In Calcutta, as in the cities of Upper India, the illumination on the great Dewali festival destroys most of them. Hence the illumination probably, in its origin. The passion of these poor minute beings for light is proverbial in the East, and has been the theme of no end of poets and poetasters. They prove their devotion unto death. Like the fabled Phœnix, they commit suicide in flame—expiring on the breast of their love. Thus they die in vast numbers. The massacre is completed by the cold weather which soon after sets in.

The most astonishing custom mentioned to-day was the carnival of the women held on the last day of the month of Kartik. Doctor RAM CHUNDRA, with a patriotic regard for the credit of his own native place, denied it as regards Muktagacha, but he could not relieve the country, confining it to the more upland and jungly parts. On that evening—on which metropolitan Bengal, with more civilised rites, worships the Indian Mars turned to a silken knight—the Garos, Haichongs, Rajbansis and other hill men descend to the plains for fun. The orgies are held in every house, but they rage most at the Rajbaris—the greater landlords being locally "Rajas." The women of the hillmen join the ladies in nude dances and voluptuous gestures and songs and wild revelry.

Now I am on the subject of curious customs, I may as well add some derived from reliable sources. By curious customs I mean, without prejudice, such as do not exist among us. One cannot help staring at a novel practice, but unless it is gross or revolting or absurd on the face of it, we have hardly a right to condemn it. To ridicule it, is rank bad taste. All customs arise in the circumstances of a country: often out of the necessities of the people. They are thus the most authentic memorials of their life—as good as historical documents. Inquiry into conflicts of curiosities in customs and manners has always been a favorite study with the enlightened. Less attention, however, has been given to interprovincial varieties—to mark the difference of practice on the same subject in different parts of the same countries or among different communities of the same people. The interest of the inquiry is obvious —its importance cannot be exaggerated. Without it there is no true knowing—no thorough grasping of a people.

To our West Bengal notions, in East Bengal the relations between the sexes seem changed —those between a man and his elder sister-in-law (wife's sister) are entirely reversed. On the banks of the Hooghly she is respected, but with no abject trembling deference. On the contrary, the intercourse is free and easy, and a good deal of latitude of converse and conversation is allowed between them. Interchange of pleasantries between them is one of the enjoyments of the Hindu's married life. It is certainly one of the prime attractions of a young bridegroom's earlier years at his father-in-law's. It serves to lighten the dreary years of betrothal rather than marriage—the period of probation following the formal union and completed in the actual consummation—during which the girl-wife progresses to maturity. No such thing in the severe East. There is unknown the poetry of the Western marital existence. There all familiarity is interdicted. For there the sister-in-law takes rank with the mother-in-law. Catch any romantic young man irreverently speaking to his wife's elder sister and his reputation is gone, as hers too unless she took offence at the unheard of liberty! She does not even make her appearance before her brother-in-law. The right, prevalent in our part of the country, of chaffing between such relations, is not only not recognised in the East, but is reckoned a great barbarity.

All the wife's elder kinsfolk are regarded

with particular respect. Her elder brother shares the distinction of her elder sister. The *Bargiré*, as he is termed, is the most favoured relation. Of course, the Tipperahs in this follow the Bangals, as the Eastern Bengalis are, without particular opprobrium, called by them, as indeed they call themselves.

Such differences in custom may be found throughout the Continent. I may fitly end this subject by citing a custom of the far West towards the Middle Land of Manu, in Upper India. In Hindostan, specially in and about Bundelkund, the younger sister—I do not mean the wife's younger sister, but the younger sister in the ordinary sense—is the revered relation. This may excite surprise as something novel, but I hope no reproach. To me it seems a most beautiful custom. Herein is the romance of Hindu life! Every man bows down to his younger sister. What an anomaly that, among such a people, it should ever have been customary to massacre the daughters at their birth!

The truth is, that it is the very consideration in which daughters were held that led to their wholesale murder.

I have come upon a rather interesting piece of information. It is in respect of the locality of a custom I had heard of from my childhood. It was a common remark with our countrymen of the banks of the Hooghly, when airing their superiority over our brethren of East Bangal, that in the East even Brahman widows were accustomed to eat dried *koi* fish roe, or rather to season their cookery with it. I have been inquiring for a long time to ascertain whether it was a fact or a mere calumny. I was repeatedly assured by my countrymen of the West, but Eastern Bengalis always professed ignorance. Today UDAY told me incidentally that beyond the Fenny river, in Chittagong, the Brahman widows eat fish. They give a reason for it, saying that virgin widows—girls who lose their husbands before puberty—might eat fish without sin. In reality, all widows eat it without distinction. In that quarter, they cure and pound shrimps to powder and use it as seasoning and as a welcome substitute in the absence of fresh fish. This substantially accounts for the roe story. Still the *chingri* powder is not *koi* roe. Nor is there any *koi* to speak of in the South. I suspect the *koi dimbo* must be used in Sylhet, which abounds in this fish.

[*Diary of the 7th November 1884, concluded.*]

From New Town to Kasba is ten miles, thence to Nyanpur six miles, and thence to Comillah sixteen miles—says Dewan RAJ MOHAN MITRA, who is now with me. * * *

At dinner, conversation turned on the meanness of these people. Mention was made of one of the favorites who has been here before but did not think it necessary to be polite so long as he hoped that the efforts of himself and his brother intriguers would keep me out of the state. On his present visit too he has been unceasing in his endeavours to poison the Maharaja against me and otherwise to prevent my installation in office. Of course, he can never imagine that I can be serious in my desire to return home as quickly as possible, or that I am not at all anxious for the place, any more than he can understand that, if I show signs to the contrary, it is simply in polite and loyal response to the extreme graciousness of language in which His Highness's offer is couched, the handsome, even extravagant terms in which he speaks of my former services to this state and of myself as the ablest and most accomplished man whom he has come across from Agartala to Brindaban! Be that as it may, directly this Daccaite realises the fact that the Maharaja is determined to have me and that the very papers of appointment are ready and in the press, he is all submission. The other day, before the Maharaja himself, in answer to my usual formal inquiry about the day of his arrival, he apologised to me for not having been able, in consequence of the darkness of the night, to wait on me on his way up to Old Agartala! Darkness of night, indeed! Why, the man wanted to learn at Old Agartala how matters stood with respect to me at court before he would think me worthy of courtesy or even give me my dues as a Brahman! Was it dark on the previous occasion—nay, two previous visits—both on coming and going away? But enough of these shameless louts!

LAST DAYS AT AGARTALA.

Monday, 1st December, 1884.—I have been suffering from a severe cold. On Saturday His Highness sent a pressing invitation to see him that evening which I was obliged to decline, but promised to strive next day and only hoped His Highness might permit me to visit him in the day. Accordingly at 1 'O'clock at night His Highness's reply came telling me to see him in the morning, which I did. That is, I started at half past 10, reached the Rajbari at about a quarter past 11, and saw the Maharaja a quarter or so later. His Highness came upon me in Bara Thakur's room accompanied by his Secretary. Several letters and papers were laid on the table, and my opinion on each matter was required.

* * * *

A letter from the Native Committee for the reception of Lord RIPON and for a suitable memorial was read by the Secretary. The movement is headed by Maharaja KOMUL KRISHNA, Nawab ABDOOL LUTEEF and the Rev. Dr. K. M. BANERJEE. I also, from my own private correspondence, informed His Highness that Mr. W. C. BONNERJEA and Kumar INDER CHUNDER SINGH are working most zealously in the matter. I am sure Messrs. GHOSE and PALIT of the bar were seconding them heartily. In fact, "it is the cause—it is cause, my soul!" though not in the Shakespearean sense.........

By order I send a sowar to Comillah to wire the following telegram from the Maharaja of Tipperah to Nawab ABDOOL LUTEEF Khan Bahadoor—

"Although following the custom of my family I would not be party to any foreign movement, far less embroil myself in the passions of politics, the Viceroy's business is an exception. Lord RIPON has so endeared himself to the Princes and People of Asia that it were churlish in any one to refuse any tribute to him, on this, that, or the other punctilio or plea of prudence. I accept your invitation, therefore, and thank you for this oportunity of testifying my high sense of the noble Marquess' invaluable services to the Imperial Crown and his unfeigned zeal on behalf of the millions subject to his influence."

Thursday, 11th December, 1884.—Yesterday was kept here as a Ripon Jubilee, in honor of the retiring Viceroy. The public offices were closed. In the evening, a grand Durbar was held by His Highness the Maharajah, who took his seat on an ivory state chair under a canvas awning, among his nobles and people. Unfortunately he fell ill under the unusual excitement and strain and could not continue long in his seat, which, however, he did not leave till the meeting had heard two short speeches at least on Lord RIPON'S Government.

Friday, 12th December.—Yesterday I was

asked to telegraph an account of the Ripon Durbar to the Press and to the Viceroy. This responsible and difficult duty I discharged as well as I could. I drew up an account of the Agartala meeting commencing with its origin in the Maharaja's regard from the beginning for the retiring Viceroy. It looked nice enough, but it was formidable for length. So I cut it down to admissible proportions. The most trying part of the business was the telegraphing to the Viceroy. Great tact and delicacy were required to avoid giving offence or making a tomfoolery of the whole business. I managed it thus. Instead of sending an account of the demonstration to the Viceroy, the Maharaja sent a parting message to Lord RIPON (whom he had seen on his return from the Brindabun pilgrimage) expressive of his high regard for His Excellency both as ruler and as man and for Lady RIPON as a worthy consort, and of his prayer for a safe voyage and good wishes for here and hereafter. This was followed by the following message

"*From* DR. SAMBHU CHUNDER MOOKERJEE,
Agartala.

"*To* THE PRIVATE SECY. TO THE VICEROY,
Calcutta.

"It might interest His Excellency to know that this Border country in the East shares the universal gratitude to his Lordship for the justice and wisdom of his administration and has joined in the demonstration. Yesterday was kept up in Independent Tipperah as a jubilee in his honor. The Maharaja has always felt the highest regard for him. When in 1881 all India, thratened with the abrupt close of a promising career, was wiring constant enquiry, the Maharaja quietly vowed to his gods. So sacrifices were offered to the Guardian Deity of Tipperah on the Viceroy's recovery. Yesterday the public offices were closed and there were illuminations and music and rejoicing in honor of the Viceroy. His Highness held a grand

Durbar of his nobles, officers and people, including British subjects staying here, at which the merits of the Viceroy's administration were extolled. A sacrifice to the gods has also been ordered for the safe return home of his Lordship and her Ladyship."

This evening went to take my final leave of the Maharaja, but to my ill luck found him unwell. So he has been ever since the meeting, as he told me. I was for bidding my last *ashirbad*, but he wished to have another interview.

Saturday, 13th December.—Called again on the Maharaja at old Agartala. Heard he was still unwell, and indeed found him worse than before. He was panting, and was surrounded by drugs, indeed plastered over with Belladonna and the whole Pharmacopœia, though the treatment had done him no good. How I wished to relieve him by scraping out his plasters and throwing them and the medicines in the room out of the window! * * * *

After midnight I got my discharge, God bless the Maharaja! No sleep till morn when one has to prepare for going home! Col. SIB SING came and found me sitting up with His Highness's work at half past 2 in the morning.

THE LAST RETURN.

Sunday, 14th December.—Started from New Town at about half past 6. Reached Mugra Rajbari in an hour or so by *palki*, accompanied by sepoys, and a lot of followers and sightseers, AODAN SINGH Orderly on elephant, leading, an officer on foot on each side of me, followed by my servant LAKIR Khansama on horseback, Mr. Deputy Registrar BANERJEE coming through the tortuous Howrah by boat, and from time to time coming upon us, and PITAMBER SINGH Orderly bringing up the rear with other boats laden with luggage and effects. Talking with my companions or with villagers met on the route, I scarcely perceived the distance. Received at the office by all the officials headed by Dewan

DOORGA PRASAD GUPTA, Tehsildar KALI PRASANNA SEN, Tehsildar (former) GAUR MOHAN BARMAN and others numbering 25 to 30, all coming down to my feet and pinching the dust of them though encased in thick woollens. Deputy Collector KALI KUMAR CHAKRAVARTI soon after appeared, to exchange greetings on more equal terms. Among the officers and staff I remarked only one Brahman.

DURGA PROSAD would have kept me at the Rajbari, and proposed to make arrangements for my dinner, but I was alarmed at the thought of living within easy reach of a recall. So I hastened to my launch in the Teetas. I was carried in my palki through fields and waste lands and round water-courses. Passing by a field of mustard in flower I inhaled a most delightful perfume, more grateful, because fresh, than the costliest Gazipore.

Monday, 15th December.—We came to Gokarna at about 9 in the morning. An hour or so after, on the way down met a country boat with the wellknown semicircular roofing of split bamboo, bearing the ruler of India east of the Megna. The Collector Political is making his gubernatorial tour, and just now coming from Brahmanberia, I presume, to Nabiganje, for inspection. The vessel, more snug than roomy, could not well hold a full Collector—the whole —man, with his traps, and it was not put to the trial. As, after the good people at home in the Emerald Isle who allot the best quarters in the house to the pigs, the health and appearance of the solid-leather portmanteau and the shining dressing-case could not be allowed to suffer by exposure, I saw the great man, in whose presence Rajas and Bahadoors trembled, in part protected by the curved shed, stretched on his Procrustean bed of an uneasy chair, his nether limbs sticking out in the open air. That shows how ill we are served in the country : for the commonest comfort you must go to the provincial capital or the still more distant metropolis ; Mr. Collector could not get a decent boat without sending to Dacca. I am sorry to be caught in my superior accommodation and equipment, thoroughly provided. I thought he hid himself with his newspaper broadsheet on seeing us playing at chess and smoking away out of our long snake-pipes. I do not blame his irritation. The contrast was too much for human nature. But I am not to blame, and I dare say he will soon recover his equanimity. At all events by the time he becomes one of the Principal Secretaries or the Lieutenant-Governor, I hope he will not remember that he ever was packed in a Bengal wherry on an Eastern river.

First sighted the well-known steeple at Nabinagar at about 2 P. M. At 4 P. M., on the right saw a field of shining stars as it were—the most beautiful sight of the kind I ever beheld. It could not be Sarsa or Til, for the plants are taller. Nor were they safflower, for these flowers were yellow while safflower is more red. The boatmen said they are flax—*sone* or *sunn*

—or, as they said, what they made rope of for rigging ships.

It is near evening, and they say we are in sight of the Megna.

We pole on till half past 7, when we reach Marchekandi where they would stop. We are for proceeding further, as far as possible, but it is not considered safe to venture beyond to-night. Even if we succeeded in passing Chorpara by this evening, still we would be scarcely safe. Our halt for the night would be on dangerous ground, or rather waters. In fact, the whole Megna is peopled on both banks by suspected Mahomedans. This Marchekandi is a rather considerable place and lots of boats are congregated here for safety. Still we are too near the Megna, and all night we are kept up by fear of pirates. I have disposed my men for an encounter in the event of the enemy entering appearance.

Tuesday, 16th December.—Left our moorings at dawn to launch ourselves on the great

Megna, now shrivelled up considerably. The great river was calm like a stagnant pool, not a ripple to break the dead level of water, nor a whiff of air to tempt the mariner to bring out his canvas from its hole in the hold. We dragged our slow length along, poling, but for the most part *gooning*, till in the afternoon we sighted the steeple of the Nags of Barodi in Sonargong—the only artificial landmark for miles in the surrounding country since we left the Nabinagar temple. I wonder the Surveyor-General's map does not note these steeples. Towards evening, I espied another minar, on the same side. What can it be? The sailors said it was the steeple of Panam. Before sunset, we entered Minakhali, not without hesitation, for there is very little water. At the mouth the streamlet is divided into two channels. That close to Baidyabazar we did not attempt, but entered the other one. Slowly wending our way, we reach the old channel of the Brahmaputra, in which we stop.

Wednesday, 17th December.—Going to bed after 1 O'clock I rose at 4-50 this morning, and ordered the mariners up. It was cruel to disturb the poor fellows doubled up cozily within their slender beddings, but I am in no mood for procrastination. And after idling for a whole month, during which they have only calculated demurrage against me, surely they ought to show some alacrity by way of thankful return. Nevertheless, they show no disposition to leave their beds. I am at them, however, setting LAKIR and my Sepoys upon them till they awake, arise, and be at their work, and the boat is fairly moved out of its moorings.

We slowly descend down the decayed Brahmapootra straight towards the Dhuleswari. The passage through Bandar is not now navigable. We are on the old channel of the great river which once swept past Sonargong in all its glory. The Brahmapootra now noisily bounds past Serajgunge through the Jumoona to join the Ganges below Goalundo. Hence the former course, which takes a sudden turn through the country eastward, defining as it proceeds the Southern boundary of the District of Mymensing, to fall into the Megna at Bhoirub Bazaar, was reduced in force and volume. The passage through Sonargong, which I take to be the older course—more ancient than even the stream that meets the Megna at Bhoirub Bazaar—has long, long been obsolete. Yet, at this part, I see it in unexpectedly good form and condition, whatever may be its state above the ruins of Sonargong city. The old bed—in its grander proportions—may still be distinctly traced between mutually distant parallels of answering forest trees on both sides, but the greater part is now mere sandbank, high and dry, with scarcely any vegetation to speak of, the remainder—a narrow minimum—being water. Although thus the great Brahmapootra, in its original course, has dwindled down to its lowest depth and smallest breadth, it is still a respectable dry-season stream, a goodly river, as good, in fact, as the Teetas—at places as broad as the Bhagirathi at Moorshedabad. In the rains, it doubtless beats the Moorshedabad river by several breadths.

The sun rises as it set last evening—a glorious spectacle!—a study in colour which would baffle all the TURNERS!—to my Bengali imagination a red hot gold plate for a dish of odoriferous Himalayan rice boiled in saffroned butter for the table of Indra, the highest of the gods!

We have reached the confluence of the many waters in the neighbourhood of Naraingunje!

Leaving Naraingunje in the distance to the right, we cross in south-westerly direction over to the opposite bank, still busy with the annual Fair held on the sandy beach, down to the water's edge. The combined waters of the Dhaleswari and the Lakhya, and of the slender Brahmapootra, constitute a goodly prospect—an ample but irregular-shaped liquid plain extending in front of the barracks of Peace on its edge on *terra firma*. To our right is a vast arc traced by the giant thatched warehouses for storing jute in, the long huts for marts of agricultural produce in general, and the brick houses and factories—with lofty chimneys sending up smoke to the skies—of the Europeans in and about Naraingunje. The scene is enlivened by the numerous boats and sloops and steam launches and other equipages—of convenience, comfort or luxury—of commerce. Now a barque winds round the sands from Naraingunje towards Dacca and again a statelier river goddess—my old love, *Princess Alice* herself—from the latter city steams down the Dhaleswari. While tiny craft—water gigs propelled by fiery ponies rather than horse power—are running backwards and forwards from shore to shore. The *Princess Alice* flies at a vigorous rate, now unencumbered by the heavy company of flats. I wonder what she is about. Possibly, she is going to fetch up a flat or two, for attendance on her passage to Goalundo. The whole is an exceptionally busy port for humdrum halting Bengal. As we near land, the long stretch of sheds of the Fair on the opposite bank gain in distinctness on the eye. As the enchantment of distance fades away, they appear in all their naked hideousness, being only structures of dry bamboo and bamboo matting, improvised for the occasion without any effort at symmetry or neatness, and beyond the most distant dream of colour. By 8-30 in the morning, we reach the bank and stop.

I send up a party on a reconnoissance. They are not only to bring information about the Fair but also to make arrangements for a run to the ruins of Rampal, the ancient capital of ADISUR and the SEN Rajas. The old lake there, on whose bank the tree is said to stand which was revived by the random touch of the spiritualised grass and corn offering of the five Aryan Rishi emigrants from Kanouj from whom the Brahman aristocracy of Bengal are all descended, is fit pilgrimage for a Koolin Brahman.

I hear the sound of a tomtom. A messenger leads the drummer, proclaiming the Fair at an end and directing the merchants and traders to shut up shop and break up camp, denouncing punishment if they don't remove their sheds and goods with themselves by tomorrow morning.

While my men are gone on shore for enquiry, I employ the interval in making some observations on the localities of these parts and taking

A FEW NOTES ON THE

GEOGRAPHY & CARTOGRAPHY

OF

EAST BENGAL.

We want a good map. I have examined many, but have found not one satisfactory. The Surveyor-General's map on the large scale is defective in many respects. Not only are the names frequently misspelt, but they are as often misplaced as not. I refer to the minor places of course. Besides this confusion, many important names do not even appear at all. The plan is answerable, in a great measure, for this contemptuous treatment of geographical notables. It is, for instance, a great mistake not to mention the Pergannas, which are not only in use in official records, at least in the transactions of the people, but which form the basis of popular geography. The wellknown names of Bikrampore, Chunderdeep, &c., which frequently occur in the conversation of the people, are nowhere. The different designations of the same place are rarely noted. The older maps are good in this respect. Thus Captain TAYLOR'S Post Office map (founded on TASSIN), for instance, has "Suwarra or Nusseerabad *or Mymensing*"; "*Bulloah or Noacally*"; "*Contay or Hidjelee.*" The Surveyor-General's map, if I remember aright, gives Sudharam as another name for Noakhali, but omits Bhulluah. TAYLOR not only shows Lucknow but Constantia—General MARTIN'S place—also. I doubt whether the Surveyor-General's people would recognise such a private place. There is not a more important minor place in these parts than Baidyabazar where the Minakhali joins the Megna, but it is ignored by the Surveyor-General's map. Instead of it, we have Haria, of which we never hear while Baidyabazar is on every lip. Although the ruins of old cities like Sonargaon and Agartala are noted, existing monuments are generally passed over in silence. "The Raja's two-storied house" at New Agartala is named in full, but the Rajbari and muts at Comillah do not appear. The residences of the old Tipperah Viziers at Singer Bil, of the ROYS of Kaitala, of the Dewans of Beetghar, and of PADDO LOCHAN Dewan, all in Pargana Noornagar, of the older Dewans, and of the Moulvis in the Pargana of Meherkool, some of them imposing structures, and all substantial, are, of course, not to be found in these large maps on the scale of four miles to the inch. These edifices do not deserve contemptuous treatment because they are private. In a land of thatched houses, mostly miserable huts, they are of great geographical importance. They take rank as landmarks. They are the first-class landmarks, in fact. For here there are no prominent natural features even ; no lasting hill ranges nor mountain peaks. Such physical features as the country possesses, are not very pronounced. In a land of corn, reed and grass, there are not many trees to speak of; and such as there are, they are liable to be cut down or to decay or to fall down and be swept away by water. But if any delicacy might be felt about incorporating private buildings in the official atlas of the Government of India, there could be none in respect of structures which, from time and popular renown, have virtually become public monuments—national institutions as it were. Such are the temples of Panam, Baradi, Nabinagar and Sultanpore. There are no more important landmarks in the country worthy of inclusion in the cartography of this part than the steeple of Baradi and that of Nabinagar. You will look for either of them in the Surveyor-General's chart in vain.

THE DHALESWARI FAIR.

December 17.

This Fair is rather a venerable institution. In a country in transition, it is more than a hundred years old. It is the most important gathering of the kind in East Bengal. The Fair at the bathing site on the Brahmapootra at Nangulband is a child's play to it. It has, however, long since passed its meridian, its grand climacteric, and is now on the sere and yellow leaf. Of late years, owing to the opening of new marts and the improvement of old ones, above all, to the augmentation and improvement of means of communication as well as to the growing habit of locomotion, it is going down in public interest and, of course, in its splendour. The same causes will prove disastrous to all the older gatherings of this description. Formerly, this Fair supplied the wants not only of the immediate locality, or the neighbouring Parganas of Sonargong-Moheshurdi, or the adjacent Districts of Tipperah and Noakhali and Backergunje, but of more distant Mymensing and far off Sylhet and Assam. In those days, moreover, people provided for their wants of a whole year. Now-a-days, they are under no such necessity ; buying when they want—without undertaking the many responsibilities, as without incurring any of the risks, of storing. They can resort to nearer marts which have since risen in the interior, or even, if necessary, proceed to more distant ones in less time than they formerly could come in to this. The lion's share of the merchandise at this Fair is taken up by tradesmen, wholesale and retail, of the whole of East and part of North Bengal. They were obliged to find and to lock up capital for their entire investment for the year. They are now wiser, as they can afford to be. They can buy here, there, everywhere, according to need, or the local consumption of their stores. The Sylhet shopkeeper who was wont to make his purchases for the year here, can now buy wholesale in Sylhet itself perhaps; if not, can procure many things from neighbouring Assam when required; at the worst, may order up goods from Calcutta or even proceed at a cheap rate there by steam and choose for himself. If a man of any character, he may even get credit more easily or on better terms at a permanent port and emporium than at an annual commercial mart. This year the Fair is in one notable respect poorer than ever. The exhibitors are gradually falling off from the growing difficulty experienced in the profitable disposal of their wares. This year the Oswals have absented *en masse*, and the Oswal element is a great factor in this traffic.

The ground belongs to two Shaoo families—headed respectively by a boy named Ramnath and my friend "Digu Babu," as he is familiarly called. The rent charged by them is not light—twelve annas for one square *nal* of ground—a few yards—the sheds being made by the exhibitors themselves. It is worth trying, perhaps, if by reducing the rate they could not keep up the institution for some time to come. The causes of decadence are, I fear, too deep-seated.

I suppose the Dhaleswari and the Lakhya are, like the Megna, modern streams. In the last century they could scarcely have been of much importance. The Booree Ganga is more than two centuries old. Possibly, it was the Old Ganges before the river took its present course to the South. The name seems to point to this fact. The Dhaleswari was then a branch of the greater river, issuing from it and falling into it. So the Lakhya, deriving its water from the Brahmapootra, recouped it, unless it paid tribute to the Ganges

—the Old Ganges, now Booree Ganga. The Brahmapootra appears to have descended from Mymensing through Sonargong and Moonsheegunje and Bikrampur, and joined the Ganges at its mouth to the north of Faridpur, or rather Backergunje District, the combined waters forming the short but very broad Megna and falling into the sea. I say rather Backergunje, because the mouth of the present Pudda is higher up to the north than the old course which formerly formed the southern boundary of the present Faridpur District. The old bed of the Ganges may be still distinctly traced in that quarter. It is named in the Surveyor-General's map as the old Pudda and Pudda Nuddee. The Kirtinassa—now the Ganges or Pudda—is a modern stream so called for destroying the monuments—Kirti—of the famed magnates of these parts, CHAND ROY and KEDAR ROY. The Brahmapootra being diverted towards Ulukandi formed the present long river Megna, while the Brahmapootra joining the Pudda by way of the Jumuna has since weakened the river in the direction of Ulukandi.

Intending to visit Rampal, I sent for a conveyance. In the map there is a direct road from this beach right through Bullal Bari, Rampal and Bajrajogini to the south. There are no wheeled vehicles for the simple reason that there are no roads. No box or chair borne on men's shoulders is to be had for either love or money. There is one apology of a palki for sale at the Fair, but it has no bottom, to say nothing of other imperfections. KUMUD NATH and LAKIR returned disappointed and dejected. For my part, I was not prepared to abandon the hope of accomplishing my long cherished wish, how I did not know. There must be some Somebodies here or about here who had a palki, said I. Tewari, the Inspector of Police in attendance at the Fair, one of Sir ASHLEY EDEN'S lucky dogs, who was at Baraset when EDEN was King there—being applied to, offered the valuable suggestion that the Zemindar's office might help us to get bearers. But what was the good of importing coals to Newcastle? I had bearers enough and to spare—a whole boatful of the Lord Jagannath's elect, in all the glory of ecclesiastical paint. However, my people set out again and returned with the gospel of success. KUMUD NATH had called on the Dewan of the Shaoo Zemindar, BEPIN Baboo, son of the late RAMNARAYAN SHAW. He is a nice young man of substance apparently, the Dewan—for the master is a minor—who, on hearing of me as the Maharaja's minister, immediately took the greatest interest in the matter. He offered to come and visit me at once but was prevented by the arrival of a lot of guests. He said he would come in the afternoon, and ordered a quantity of provisions for me—an order which KUMUD NATH prevailed upon him to withdraw. After enquiry, he sent one of his orderlies, a Pahalwan who had formerly been to Agartala, over to me to say that a palki might be had from the house of his minor principal. Immediately I sent my bearers to bring it and keep it ready for me.

"Could we but know
The land that ends our dark, uncertain travel,
Where lie those happier hills and meadows low,—
Ah, if beyond the spirit's inmost cavil,
Aught of that country could we surely know,
Who would not go?

"Might we but hear
The hovering angels' high imagined chorus,
Or catch, betimes, with wakeful eyes and clear,
One radiant vista of the realm before us,—
With one rapt moment given to see and hear,
Ah, who would fear?"

RUINS OF RAMPAL,

THE HINDU CAPITAL OF BENGAL.

I wanted a guide, only. My palki-men are strangers to these parts, indeed distant Orissans. This difficulty was easily overcome by the Pahalwan volunteering to accompany me. I told him to come after a couple of hours. I went through my personal duties and, after dinner, left.

KUMUD NATH, after vain efforts to secure so much even as a beggar's horse, had given up the trip, but I would not hear of it. I prophesied the shame and mortification that must be his portion, if he threw away such an opportunity of visiting the famed Hindu antiquity of Bengal; and, after all, the way was short. He had been scared away by people speaking of the distance and the difficulties of the way. I pointed out to him, by the Surveyor-General's 4 inches to the mile map, how baseless was the idea of distance, at any rate. Bullal Bari was not quite two miles off! and Rampal proper not quite a mile from there! The difficulties must be an equally contemptible scarecrow which could frighten away only Calcutta Baboos from such a poor but promising enterprise. In fine, the picture of the arduousness and even hazardousness of the journey, as I shrewdly guessed, was a devise of these people, at which our own assisted, at once to escape the search, in right earnest, for conveyance, and preserve the reputation of the place, and finally to leave me a drop of consolation under disappointment. He then consented to brave it on foot.

We left our aquatic camp at 3 P.M. It was with no ordinary sense of relief that I stept on land, after so many days of durance vile on board. Leaving the sand-bank behind and a shed temple or abbey to the left, we got upon *terra firma*, and wended our way through a Bengali village. Indeed, we cut right through a lot of bamboo-made country bullock-carts scattered in the courts about its neat little well-mopped shed homes—which, for the first time, gave me an idea of the kind of houses in which our Agartala Amla live in Bikrampore and elsewhere, —at the back of which lay some goldsmiths' forge. I came upon the house of BEPIN Baboo. It is a rather imposing residence of the old style, showing that the family of the late RAMNARAYAN was opulent from a long period, that is, before the rise of the British. Sweeping past the house, I rode through the fringe of a pond where I was overwhelmed by a horrible stench. Surely, that was the identical Bykunt of JAFER KHAN—the purgatory of fiscal tyranny through which the defaulting landholders were wont to be drawn in that wretch's Nawabate. It would seem as if all the filth and excreta of ages were gathered there. How people manage to exist and even to flourish in the vicinity! It required the compensation of the perfume of several mustard fields in flower to efface the unpleasantness. The beauty of a Mussulmani of the agricultural class also disposed me to good humour.

BEPIN had had another house built for him in the modern style, on larger and more expensive proportions, certainly not grander, a little less than half a mile off. But he could not remove there owing to a warning. He was prevented by a dream in which he was informed that the river would move away.

The villages on our route are peopled by lower class Hindus and Mahomedans. No hideous pot-bellied dirty urchins, encircled by a string round the waist for clothing, or bandaged with stinking amulets and charms, such as Bengali hamlets in some parts abound in, met us on the way. The children we saw are far from ugly. Many possess clear complexions and fine features. Whether I was fortunate in having gathered for my inspection the best specimens, or not, I certainly found good grounds for concluding this secluded region a land of beauty. The Mahomedans specially have the advantage in this respect. I espied among some poor families living in mean thatched huts beside shady trees on the banks of a village pond, some particularly handsome fair women and children. How they come by their clear complexion and regular features, is a wonder. The problem is one in the ethnology of Bengal. The late JOHN LANG, lawyer and *litterateur*, the founder-editor of the *Mofussilite*, English newspaper at Meerut, in his Indian Travels—a book which deserves to be better known—oracularly avers that colour is no criterion of gentility in India. That is too sweeping a generalization, which Mr. LANG tries to support by the most unlucky illustrations. It is by no means an absurd remark, however. Its author must have continually lighted upon proofs in its favour. Yet it is far from absolutely true—showing how difficult it is for foreigners to form correct views of matters Indian. Complexion is not an accident. It is only among the higher classes, whether Hindu or Mussulman—the representatives of Aryan emigration in the one case, and the representatives of Aryan and Semitic in the other—that we have ordinarily a right to expect much personal beauty. Some tribes seem to present a puzzle. The Sonar Banias, who form such an important part of the Hindu community of Calcutta and Hoogly and the neighbouring places, are, specially in their women, a good-looking people. From some observations and enquiries I made many years ago, I found that the Joogies, if they did not as a rule suffer from poverty as the Sonar Banias are rich, might put forward the same claim. The Shaoos of Dacca might be equally distinguished, but I have no knowledge. They are a respectable class who have nothing in common, except perhaps remote origin, with the Soorees of the Calcutta district. But even these publicans have no low caste aspect and indeed shame many of the ill-favoured classes that assert superiority over them. The Kapali is another of the "suppressed" castes that have in Calcutta risen to wealth. The Kapalis in town scarcely retain the tradition of their original calling in the country. The wealthy live in style; as they drive past you in their elegant broughams or lordly barouches, they are indistinguishable from the rich of other classes. But even their poorest castemen in the far interior are not ugly. A protracted trial at the Agartala sessions at which I presided, in which a whole Kapali hamlet was implicated in the murder of a girl, gave me an unequalled opportunity for seeing the Kapalis of that part of the country. They impressed me favorably. The principal defendant was a beauty, with a fine fair complexion, and it was with a heavy heart that I convicted and passed sentence on her. Luckily, the circumstances proved did not amount to absolute murder, so that I was spared the capital responsibility. All these several classes, I have no doubt, are of Aryan descent. The Joogees claim a high Jogi—twice-born ascetic—origin. The Kapalis might do the same; their designation is in their favour.

These Moonsheegunje Mussulmans, still retaining such a proportion of good looks and fine complexion, seem to be descended either from superior Hindu converts or superior foreign Mussulmans. In the former case, however, they could scarcely have so degenerated in *status* and occupation. The mere tradition of caste would have preserved them in their high estate, at least from grovelling in the lowest mire. I conclude them to be of *villayeti*—extra-Indian—descent. The Mussulmans, without the discipline of that passive but powerful aristocratic feeling which is not absent in any class of Hindu society, are, when power or external means and education fail, apt to decay. Thus I found at Agartala that the learned

Hakeem who went from the West and lived as a grandee at the Court of the late Maharaja KRISHNA KISOR MANIKYA—the present Maharaja's father—having married beneath him there, is now represented by a son who has no pretensions to his father's social grade. He is a fine strapping youth, with a manly heart I dare say, as with a manly presence, but the poor fellow cannot write or read, nor will he plough. He draws a pension from the Rajbari, and, for the rest, contents himself with the exploits of a village Nimrod. His son will, of necessity, be a cultivator direct. Such a deterioration is next to impossible among the Hindus, showing the continual need of careful selection for marriage and of the influences of education and property for our Mahomedan brethren. In Tipperah, there are many other instances of fallen families—of Mirzas and Begs employed in husbandry or as policemen and messengers. Here, in Moonsheegunje, these rural Mussulmans had probably Mogul or

Pathan ancestors. We are in the neighbourhood of the old Mogul capital of Bengal. But this part of the country was the refuge of the Pathans before the conquering Moguls—one reason of the preponderance of the Mahomedan element in the population of these countries.

The very cattle, though ill-fed and worked to death, are a better breed than the ordinary Bengali cow.

In three quarters of an hour after leaving the fleet, we come upon a trench. It is the trench of the great Hindu—whether Vaidya or Kayastha is now disputed between the rival castes—King BULLAL SEN. Here commences the work which goes a great way off. Or rather, here is one end of a work of considerable extent. For, it is the moat of the monarch's palace. Except for its associations, the ditch has nothing to recommend it or to arrest the eye. Had it not been specially and specifically pointed out to me, I would scarcely have noticed it. It is not remarkable for depth.

Altogether, it has too much the air of a modest modern concern, for reverence. For all that, it may be the remains of the very moat of Bullal Bari which, having filled up by accumulation of silt, was since cleared and redug out, for purposes of possessory demarcation. It stretches out on both sides around the place, looking like the separating ditches in the villages of metropolitan Bengal. At places, however, it has a more business-like, if not formidable, appearance. We cross it by an old wooden bridge—a British work. The peculiarity of the prospect in this part of the place, is the cultivation of the plaintain. This is the principal produce of this orchard of Dacca and Naraingunje. Groves of this plant are on all sides of our way, each numbering from a thousand to three thousand thriving trees. The rival of the plantain is the sugarcane—the slender red species. The bamboo grows thick and luxuriant in innumerable clusters scarcely needing plantation. The rattan-cane is absolutely wild and abundant. The plantain, the better cultivated kinds like the *Champa*, is a fine substantial yet delicious fruit. But here only the *Kantali* or *Safri* is raised. From the vast numbers of the trees, I imagined that they were planted for their fibres for manufacturing purposes, but I saw no apparatus for extracting the fibre or signs of industry of that kind, and was told that they were cultivated for the fruit only. What a pity that our people in the East should still be eating plantains—of the *Kantali* kind and almost the *Kantali* kind only! It is a wretched fruit, of the same status as the *Anona*, and fit, like it, for the table of Santals only. In and around Calcutta, we have long since outgrown the barbarism of that dessert, thanks to our European connection from a long time! Here, among us, only widows and punctilious elders are condemned to the *Kantali*, for they will not touch any others. It is thoroughly orthodox, for it is our only ancient fruit of the kind, the only one mentioned in our

Scriptures and our classical literature—in fact, the only one that has a Sanskrit name. Our gods and kings are really to be pitied for having known no better—our Rishis, in especial, who lived principally on fruits, and had only this poor *Kantali* for a perennial staple. The up-country Rishis had to go without the fruit altogether, as even the ill-favoured but sweet and nutritious *Kantali* throve not, as it grows not to this day, in Upper-India. It is only since our country has been thrown open to foreign, above all, European enterprise, that our orchards and flower-gardens and kitchen-gardens have been vastly improved, that we have made the acquaintance of new and desirable eatables and drinkables and acquired a taste for new comforts and luxuries, as well as the means for satisfying them. Undue pretensions must be curbed: It is necessary to keep the best men and races straight, and I have never been slow to prick when required—the objects of the attention enjoying the thing and it having, by the way, a wholesome effect on the neighbours and bystanders of all camps. But the insane jealousy of the White-man I can never sympathise with. It is neither patriotic nor candid. It is simply ignorant and puerile. A moment's inward glance at the source of our most energysing ideas—the slightest inquiry into the derivation of our physical enjoyments—of what we eat or drink or wear or sleep upon or write with—what houses we live in—what furniture we use—ought to be sufficient to disabuse every honest Indian of the unfortunate prejudice. The stranger has given a substantial return. He has at any rate given you the golden *Champa* plantain—no Dead Sea apple, but with rich pulp within. It is your fault if you neglect it. Thus, in East Bengal, where his influence has been less felt, our brethren are without it. Here then is distinct room for improvement. The man that introduces in his district the exotic fruits and vegetables with which foreigners have enriched our land, will benefit at once himself and his country.

Thus we wend our way through Bullal Bari—once the moated palace of a long line of kings, now a vast intrenched area of rural cultivation and habitation. To the observant eye, it has the look of a low tableland, slightly raised above the deep rice fields at its back. Hence the cultivation is of the upland character—there are orchards and gardens of substantial trees, shady or lofty, interspersed with huts, few and far between, or a hamlet or two. And now we suddenly come upon the rice plant! For that matter, we have whole fields of it! How so? But see the end of them before our eyes! The ground on their other side is high and dry again, bearing villages protected by giant trees as by picked body-guards. These rice-fields are not continuous low plots, but slope from the sides down to the centre, still, in the height of December, filled with water, more or less. This had evidently been a vast lake—the reservoir of the Sen Kings. In fact, we are right on the very borders of the famous "Bullal Dighee"!

And the venerable and lofty Gajari tree, the most precious relic of the place as of ancient Hindudom in Bengal, rich in the homage of many centuries, stands before us in all its hoary majesty! One can hardly believe one's senses. Miraculous in origin, marvellous in growth, romance has continually gathered round the tree, until it had faded in the mind to a veritable myth. But here it is, in all its grandeur and glory, without possibility of mistake! Can it be the same on which the power of the fiery Aryan colonists—the Five Rishis from whom the Brahmans of Bengal are descended—was displayed? It has certainly all the appearance of great age. It is still in fine health, but its growth has been exhausted. It is about 80 cubits in height, but it had evidently been loftier. The Gajari is not quite the Sal *(Shorea robusta)* but another species with shorter leaves. Apart from its history, this specimen is a notable plant. It is the only tree of its kind, for the Gajari grows not in the Delta. It forks out from near the root into two heads. It bears marks of worship, being painted at the roots and lower end with vermillion. It is the resort of barren women who hanker for an interesting situation. Since the dead post for teddering the royal elephant revived under holy touch, countless fair eyes have washed the feet of the good Gajari. And now it is not only a monument of antiquity and faith but the most prominent landmark in the country within many, many miles.

The whole tract between the Dhaleswari and the Ganges—locally Kirtinasa—is classic ground—one of the earliest seats of Bengali civilization—one of the most advanced posts of the Aryan migration from the North West. In spite of the vicissitudes of civil history combining with a tropical climate acting on an alluvial soil, there are abundant traces of ancient population, wealth and power. The ground itself is high, a flat mound, presenting to the eye of the plainsman the appearance of a low hill—in reality evidencing a pulverised if not buried city.

There are remains of great public works. The present rural jungle-encompassed footpath was once a broad causeway extending from river to river, from the Dhaleswari, right through the western embankment of the great Bullal Lake, to Rajbari. And there are other roads, though less important, to be traced—all attributed to BULLAL SEN. Artificial lakes too abound. There are still some interesting villages in the neighbourhood. Bujjrojogini, with its cluster of twenty-seven odd villages, is one of the most important Hindu settlements, teeming with high caste and low caste life. Panchsar, now a rural village, was once the royal residence of the great ADISOOR.

PUBLICATIONS BY THE SAME WRITER.

CAUSES OF THE MUTINY. By A Hindu of Bengal. Edited by Malcolm Lewin, Esq., late a Judge of the Madras Sudder Court and Provisional Member of Council. London, Stanford, 1857.

MR. WILSON, LORD CANNING, AND THE INCOME TAX. By Somboo C. Mookerjee. Calcutta, 1859.

THE CAREER OF AN INDIAN PRINCESS, Her Highness the late Secundra Begum of Bhopal, K.C.S.I. By Sambhu Chandra Mukhopadhyaya. Calcutta, 1869.

"Mr. Mill asserts in his *Subjection of Women* that in India women have, on the whole, proved themselves greater administrators than men, and it is undoubtedly true that in our time the most distinguished and most successful native rulers have belonged to the sex which Mr. Mill describes as subjugated. The mother of Dhuleep Singh . . . . .
The Begum of Oudh . . . . . . The Ranee of Jhansie . . . . None among these, however, had so strong a character as the Mussulman lady who died last October, and who for twenty-one years governed Bhopal with the wit and the success of a great

statesman, or displayed her capacity for sensible, straightforward rule. Her State was not very large, not very much bigger than the Eastern Counties, and her revenue did not exceed that of the Duke of Devonshire, but still she was one of the true governing class of earth, and the facts of her career may interest our readers as well as any parochial matter. They have been recalled to our recollection by a short biography just received, in which a Kulin Brahmin of Bengal contrives in his admiration of her to insinuate some strongly depreciatory but not very unjust remarks upon our rule . . . . The author . . is a shrewd, hard-hitting critic, with no slight political ability. This, for instance, is a nearly perfect answer to Mr. Mill, much better because simpler than our own, which was that . . . . Sambhu Chandra Mookerjee says . . . . . He seems, too, thoroughly aware of the specialty of his heroine, her consciousness of masculine ability, for he quotes two or three times her . . . . . . her native apologist explains by a suggestion which strikes us as singularly shrewd. She had always, he says . . . . No one, we believe, either European or native, ever came in contact with her without a conviction that, had her sphere been but a little larger, she might have founded a dynasty or built up an empire. Her history is quoted by her native biographer as a proof that "that utter disqualifier in Asia" her sex, can be overcome by rare personal qualities . . . . .—*From a Leading Article in* "The Spectator," *London.*

This short—too short—little memoir . . . . We have said "too, short," because the very eventful life of her whom the writer styles "the best by far of all the native sovereigns of India of our time, the ablest, wisest, most enlightened and most fortunate," affords. . . . . because also, to judge from this little specimen—the author, with sufficient data before him, is capable of producing a very good biography.

In conclusion this excellent little biography is of especial interest to persons who study the relations of the British Government with the Independent Powers. —*From a Review in* "The Asiatic," *London.*

THE PRINCE IN INDIA AND TO INDIA. By An Indian. Calcutta, Berigny & Co., 1872.

The Prince in India and to India, by an Indian, is not an unpleasant book to read. With many satirical hits at the unfortunate Englishman who never fails to be the butt for the shafts of every Bengali archer, to whom he has unwarily imparted his own vernacular, and though somewhat marred by the incurable diffuseness of the Bengali, it shows throughout a truly wonderful command of the English language. The writer is justifiably severe on the miserable *fiascos*, which, as he truly says, we invariably make when we attempt anything in the way of a pageant, and he waxes eloquent....... But the main current of thought which runs through the book, is that of complaint that the Englishman does not associate more cordially with his Eastern fellow-subject, and more particularly with the Bengali. There are the two well-known pictures drawn in vivid contrast of light and shade, like one of Lord Macaulay's historical portraits—the native on the one side, a being of the tenderest sensibilities and most gushing emotions ; on the other...... .—*The Indian Observer.*

THE PRINCE IN INDIA, AND TO INDIA.—By Sambhu Chandra Mukhopadhyaya. (Trübner)—We should say that this was an interesting revelation of thoughts and feelings that prevailed among the natives of India, if we felt sure that an Oriental ever does reveal his thoughts and feelings. Some expressions, however, are, we may feel tolerably certain, genuine enough. Our author says :—

"I do not expect, as the immediate effect of the late visit of the Prince, any sudden or sweeping reforms in administration : these may come in due course ; all I anticipate—and this I have a right to expect—is a visible improvement in the tone of the Government, and of English, and ultimately Anglo-Indian, society towards the hundreds of millions of Asiatics subject to England. We believe in the reality of *tone*, in the existence of an atmosphere either suffocating or refreshing. Tone may exasperate, atmosphere may conciliate. Always important, in our case tone is all-important, for after all that is urged regarding the ill-success or unpopularity of British rule in India, the worst, the chief, almost the sole blister is caused by—a tone."

Another fault of ours, about the reality of which we may be pretty certain, is that we are not *magnificent* enough. There ought, thinks our author, to have been other great ceremonials to welcome the Prince and give him an imperial prestige than the one which accompanied his investiture with the Order of the Star of India. "I think," he adds significantly, "Indian money would have been better spent in such a valuable *Tamasha* than in *fêting* the Sultan in London." Generally the author's exposition of native feelings is profoundly interesting and expressed with great force. We may add that he shows as keen an understanding of our own politics, when his subject happens to bring him into contact with them, as could any writer of our own.—
The Spectator, *(London.)*

Messrs. Berigny & Co., Calcutta, have published a little after date, but none the worse on that account, a sketch from the pen of Sambhu Chandra Mukhopadhyaya, of the Prince of Edinburgh's doing in Calcutta and of all that was done in giving him welcome. . . . . . There is something though, and something important too, in what our author says about the sheer inaptitude of Englishmen for producing a real pageant. He literally pours waggon-loads of sarcasm upon us for our reception of Prince Alfred. . . . .

A more uncompromising piece of criticism was never offered to the public ; and now having heard the whole of our satirist's bitter satire, let us give him a little bit of advice in return. We acknowledge our inaptitude, our clumsiness, our sheer incapacity for pageantry. We never were able to make a good show in our own land or any other......But when our author tells us that the power to produce a pageant is one of the chief things required in India, we tell him that, with all respect for pageants, and all proper admission of their value, we dispute his views. We think that if the English race in India can comprehend what is involved in raising the condition of the lowest classes of the people, in developing the resources of the country, in educating the people to understand rightly their own history and the history of mankind, the story of English rule in India will be a nobler one than even that of the race of Baber to which our author appeals.

. . . .

We accept the lesson of our critic : we hope that he in return will accept ours, which is worth quite as much as his to India.—*The Friend of India.*

Lord Salisbury has found an unexpected supporter of his argument that this country is not fitted for representative institutions in Baboo Sambhu Chandra Mu-

khopadhyaya, who has just published a Memorial of the Visit of the Duke of Edinburgh to India. . . . . .
—The "Englishman."

But we have space for no more. The above, we hope, will give a fair idea of *the work, one which is, seriously speaking, worth reading*, inasmuch as it is by far the most native of the native productions we have lately seen.—From a leading article in The "Pioneer."

The *Indian Observer* lately had what it scarcely ever has—an article written in singularly bad taste............ But we totally refuse to consider the Prince's tour in this aspect, and *we commend to "Indian Observer's" attention a book recently put forth by an Indian author,* ("The Prince in India and to India") *which we briefly noticed in our local columns at the time, but which will well repay perusal by Englishmen who wish to know how such subjects strike the native mind.* . . . . . The writer's language may be occasionally a little too oriental and exuberant, but we have seldom seen several of the great Anglo-Indian questions of the day treated with a truer conception of the real facts. The charge of want of loyalty and gratitude, so commonly brought against the Bengali, seems to rankle in our author's mind. . . . .

The Bengalis have lately received, and deserved, a severe castigation from the Indian Press for their foolish self-praise, yet this is no reason why we should refuse to look on our own faults as reflected in a Bengali mirror. * * *
—From a leading article in "The Englishman."

THE EMPIRE IS PEACE: THE BARODA *COUP D'ETAT*. Being the Baroda Number of *Mookerjee's Magazine*, (New Series, edited by Sambhu

Chandra Mookerjee), Calcutta, Berigny & Co., 1875.

If we have always admired Mookerjee and his *Magazine*, we did not expect such a fine thing as his present Baroda number, even from him. Whether in point of interest, research, logic, wit, and grace of style, it can rank with the best of European productions. It is fearless in its tone, profound in its researches, precise in its arguments, happy in its expressions and exhaustive in its range. We are grateful to him for this brilliant production, and we can only express our gratitude by recommending every body to purchase a copy.—*Amrita Bazar Patrica.*

. There is ability as well as force and bitterness in the .bill of indictment drawn up against England, and it will doubtless serve its purpose of lashing into fury the enmity of many of our native fellow-subjects. We really admire the candour and boldness of the writer ; his language may be here and there exaggerated, but he has certainly hit not a few blots, and if he has done harm by exciting the passions of our foes, he has also done *us* good—just as a bitter tonic is more afficacious than a mere soothing syrup. From a leading article in the *Statesman*, (Calcutta and Bombay.)

We don't think we ever read such unmitigated outspoken criticism, verging on treason if not overstepping the boundary, as Mookerjee's Baroda number. But the style is good and the language admirable, every word flowing easy and yet each brief sentence is acutely in-incisive. As to reason or logic, they are most cleverly parodied. The writer seems to have studied Comte to some purpose and such a torrent of sophism never before carried all sober fact before it clear out of sight.—*The Athenæum and Daily News*, (Madras.)

When Baboo Sambhu Chandra Mookerjee was a young man, fresh from the Hindu Metropolitan College, the late Baboo Haris Chandra Mookerjee singled him out as a youth of great promise. Our lamented predecessor had a high opinion of Baboo Sambhu Chandra, and that distinguished journalist, Mr. Meredith Townsend, has more than once spoken of him as a man of "high political ability." The Baroda number of his *Magazine* does not belie the promises of his youth. Nothing more interesting than the Baroda number has of late emanated from the pen of a Bengalee. Baboo Sambhu Chandra Mookerjee has a personal knowledge of the courts of several Native Princes, and it would be no exaggeration to say that he knows more about their relations to our Government, than any other Bengalee that we know of. . . .—*The Bengalee.*

NOTICE

To Native Princes and Noblemen, Merchant-Princes, Planters and Zemindars, Retired or retiring Europeans, Missionary, philanthropic and other Societies, and speculators.

FOR SALE

The rent-free magnificent house and property
CLEVELAND CASTLE,
BHAGULPORE, BEHAR.

With an area of about eighty beegahs of land, the garden abounding in all sorts of fruit trees, the mangoe being the finest at the station and among the finest in the country. Bounded on the North by the Ganges, on the West by the Garden of Rammonee Thakoor, on the East by open land adjoining to that of Mr. Grant, and on the South by the public Road before the public Gardens.

Cleveland Castle was formerly the Political Residency for this part. It is situated on the crest of a neat little hill overlooking the great river and the surrounding country and commanding the finest prospect. It was built by the munificence and taste of the illustrious Augustus Cleveland, the civiliser of the tribes of the Rajmehal Hills, whose monument at the expense of the East India Company with an inscription on marble from the classic pen of Warren Hastings, First Governor-General, graces the grounds and is the object of pilgrim veneration.

This is a fine edifice, the most splendid, loftiest and as well as most finely situated, in a salubrious climate, in the whole country. It is extremely well-adapted for a mess-house, hotel, school, or family residence. There is no end of rooms in the great house, which is approached by a grand flight of steps. The out-offices are conveniently detached, being at the foot of the hill.

It is, of course, a place of great interest to intelligent travellers, including artists, and has been noticed in a variety of books.

The whole neighbourhood is full of historic remains.

Apply to
Baboo MUTTY LALL PRAMANIK,
at Messrs. PEEL, JACOB & Co.,
12, Clive Street, Calcutta.

THE

London Musical Depot.

MILITARY BAND INSTRUMENTS

BY THE CELEBRATED MAKERS

F. BESSON & CO.

LONDON.

The above are used by nearly all BANDS, of both British and Native Regiments, and have taken 42 GOLD MEDALS and AWARDS in various parts of the world. This alone is sufficient to prove their superiority.

MUSICAL INSTRUMENTS

OF EVERY DESCRIPTION.

New Catalogues now ready, Post free.

T. E. BEVAN & CO.,

13-1, Old Court House Street,

CALCUTTA.

Price Rs. 6 *post free.*

TRAVELS & VOYAGES IN BENGAL

BETWEEN

CALCUTTA & INDEPENDENT TIPPERAH.

BY SAMBHU C. MOOKERJEE.

Calcutta : *Reis & Rayyet* Office,

1, Uckoor Dutt's Lane, Wellington Street.

OPINION OF THE PRESS.

We sometimes hear the complaint that the educated natives of Bengal do not honour themselves or their country by devoting time to literary pursuits ; or, that those who do so, fail to show the ability which might be expected from them. We anticipate that this reproach will be removed, in at least one instance, shortly. We see it announced that there is about to be published a volume of miscellaneous papers, largely of travel and voyage in Bengal, by Sambhu Chunder Mookerjee. There is no one whom we know among the natives of this country who wields so graceful and correct a pen in the English language as Dr. Mookerjee. He has a wide range of thought, and a facility of expression that are not common even among our own countrymen. He must have been a diligent reader and student of classical English authors, and has largely profited by their study. He is well known through the newspaper, *Reis & Rayyet*, of which he is the Editor, and which he always turns out a readable and instructive paper; nor can we suppose that his forthcoming volume will be otherwise.---*The Indian Daily News*, Sept. 8, 1887.

Travels and Voyages in Bengal.---The Editor of *Reis and Rayyet* is about to publish a small volume of about 300 pages of travels and voyages in Bengal between Calcutta and Independent Tipperah, by Babu Shambhu Chunder Mookerjee, which, to judge by the list of contents, should prove both interesting and useful.---*The Englishman*, Sept. 8, 1887.

We understand that the editor of *Reis and Rayyet* has a small volume in the press, of about 300 pages, consisting of extracts from his Travels and Voyages in Bengal. The author is so well known to all sections of the Calcutta community, for his graceful and indeed brilliant writings, that they need no commendation from ourselves.---*The Statesman*, September 11, 1887.

Dr. Sambhu Chunder Mookerjee, the profoundly learned editor of *Reis and Rayyet*, is about to bring out a volume of about 300 pages, consisting of extracts from his Travels and Voyages in Bengal. Dr. Sambhu Chunder needs no introduction at our hands. In sarcasm, humour, purity of diction and many other excellent qualities he stands almost unrivalled in the ranks of Indian journalism. We doubt whether there is another man in India who has so mastered the English language. His magnificent and effective writings have always secured to him a high position, even amongst the Anglo-Indian writers of note. It therefore goes without saying that the incoming book will be a very interesting reading to the general public.---*The Amrita Bazar Patrika*, Sept. 22, 1887.

We have received from the office of *Reis and Rayyet*, one of the leading native newspapers of Calcutta, a most readable little *brochure* written by Baboo Sambhu C. Mookerjee, once Minister to the late Nawab Faridoon Jah, Bahadoor, Nawab Nazim of Bengal, Behar and Orissa, which gives a graphic account of the Baboo's travels to and in Independent Tipperah. Written in capital English and evidently by a gentleman of broad views and enlightened mind, the work is decidedly a valuable addition to the catalogue of English written Bengalee literature.

This book of travels should be read widely not only by English residents out here, but by our countrymen at home, for it teems with interest and teaches us far more about the fine belt of unopened country travelled through than any work of the sort written by an Englishman would have done. Baboo Sambhu Chunder Mookerjee is one of whom his countrymen may well be proud, for he writes throughout with the moderate and educated pen of a thorough gentleman.—*The Indian Planters' Gazette & Sporting News*. October 4, 1887.

Mr. S. Mookerjee, who will be readily recognised as the editor of that able little paper the *Reis and Rayyet*, dedicates his travles in Bengal to a wide circle of readers—those who know India and are unable to love her; those who love her, and do not know her; those who neither know nor love; those who being tired of India, take to travelling; foreigners who want to know, and Englishmen. The author himself is not the least tired of India, though he is a traveller by profession, we might almost say, and though he puts limits upon journeys, never caring to get very far away from Calcutta. It is not mileage, however, which makes the traveller. It is the power to observe sympathetically what is going on at each stage of a journey, and to keep his spirit about the minor inconveniences which necessarily occur by road, river, or rail. This Mr. Mookerjee does. He never loses his good humour under any set of circumstances, and what is better, he conveys a full sense of it to his pages. The reader may take a choice of journeys through Eastern Bengal to Tipperah, or to the heart of Bengal Proper, and will in each case be fully rewarded by the fruits of Mr. Mookerjee's wanderings. Perhaps the English reader will be mainly struck by the excellent English style of the writer. The author is not ashamed of his nationality ; he rejoices in being a Bengali, but at the same time he indulges in prose which has no alien trace in it. It is not the English of an educated German or Frenchman ; it is the nervous Saxon of a subject of the Empress of India. Mr. Mookerjee had special advantages in some of his journeys, especially to Independent Tipperah, whither he was called to an important official position. He was thus assured of many attentions, though, in forming accurate impressions of a country it is doubtful whether it is not better to be untrammelled with connections which frighten away the simple folk and impose reticence on them as a duty. From the notes of his journey through East Bengal, and to show how genial is his outlook, we take the following :—[Extract.]

From Dacca he went further East, and his experiences on the Megna are of a most enlivening description. He saw many visions of beauty, and Mr. Mookerjee is no niggard when he is describing something he has enjoyed seeing. Here is a sketch on his way up the river :—[Extract.]

But it is not physical beauty alone which detains our author's eye :—[Extract].

The same symptoms of material progress he notes among the boatmen on his course.—[Extract.]

Some portion of the volume has already been contributed to the *Statesman*, and will be familiar to our readers. The following description of natural effects is not known to them. We doubt whether Mr. Ruskin, or Mr. Black would accept it as a final account of the sun's rising and setting :—[Extract].—*The Statesman*, October 7, 1887.

The talented editor of *Reis and Rayyet* does not stand in need of a certificate from us for his excellent

English. His command over that language has been the cause of wonder to many Europeans. Why, in the book before us, Dr. Mookerjee *naively* confesses this: "He (Father Justin Clerici, O. C. B., the Roman Catholic priest of Noakhali) does not speak English fluently or idiomatically and expressed great surprise at my proficiency. I must have been in England, he thought." Many other European gentlemen had complimented Dr. S. C. Mookerjee on his linguistic attainments. But he is a modest man. He says that there are many more like him, as "good fish in the sea as out of it." We must add our word of praise though ours does not count for much. Natives of India who hold that the English language cannot be mastered by foreigners, will find here a refutation. But apart from its linguistic merits,the book has a value of its own. It has been a standing reproach against the natives that they do little towards laying open before the eyes of foreigners or for that matter natives also, the beauties of their country. Dr. Mookerjee has shown that there are natives who can successfully perform the task. His descriptions of natural scenery and phenomena, his portraits of the people, his dissertations on history and sociology are all evidences of a strong intellect, of keen perception and the faculty of marshalling thoughts. We commend the book "Mookerjee's Travels in Bengal" to our readers.---*The Mahratta.* October 9, 1887.

Mr. Mookerjee has been before the public for years as editor of a native paper, and as author of several books on Indian subjects. Both his way of looking at things and his way of remarking on them are original. The novel and interesting book before us is exactly what its title indicates, or, as Mr. Mookerjee says in his preface, "a book of travels at home—the journeyings of a Calcutta Bengali in Bengal Proper." "Called to office in Tipperah," he writes, "I, for the first time, in 1878, saw East Bengal. I have since been several times all through the country to that State and back, keeping notes of what struck me. Out of eight journeys in all, counting returns, here are accounts of only four---two trips to Tipperah and two trips back." The following extract from the introduction is in the author's best style, and gives in a few sentences a complete sketch of the history of Tipperah from the earliest times to the present day :—[Extract.]

The successive chapters consist of jottings made

either on boats and steamers as the author pursued his journeys by water, or as he travelled across country and took up his residence in Tipperah. While the account is all readable, there can be no doubt Mr. Mookerjee is right in calling those portions the most important which are headed "Glimpses of Life in a Hindu State," "Curious Customs," "Notes on Geography and Cartography," "The Dhaleswari Fair," and "The Ruins of Rampal, the Hindu capital." Things are described which a European would be likely to pass over, and other things are passed over which a European would notice. Much strange information is given about the social life of the people and their relations to the authorities. Old traditions are related, and a few antiquities described. Having come upon a Roman Catholic village in Tipperah, the traveller writes at considerable length, in a chatty style about "the history of Portuguese settlement in Bengal, and the introduction of artillery to the East." But nothing in the book equals the account of the ancient civilization of Hindus in those remote parts. "The whole tract between the Dhaleswari and the Ganges is classic ground."—*The Englishman*, October 19, 1887.

An interesting volume which throws a luminous light on the history of the country between Calcutta and Independent Tipperah, and recounts with entertaining freshness many incidents relating to the life, customs and manners of the people, great and small. The book is issued from the office of *Reis and Rayyet* in an attractive form, which its readable contents well deserve.—*The People's Budget and Railway Service Gazette*, (now *The Morning Post*,) October 22, 1887.

The general reader will rise from a perusal of Mr. S. C. Mookerjee's book of travels and voyages with more than expected satisfaction. The *naiveté* and charm of his pages, written with a cultivated literary taste, and in exceptionally good English, carrries the reader, without letting him feel the tedium of *ennui*, through mazes of a polished and entertaining conversation, interspersed with sketches of humorous anecdote and with the results of an experience of men and manners, and a knowledge of times past and present—a rare combinaton that will raise him in the estimation of those who know him as well as of those who read him, whether it be in a spirit of fair criticism, or from desire to learn something of the man who dedicates "this little booklet" to several and sundry, as also to Englishmen, "on whose sympathetic knowledge depends the good of the Indian myriads."

There are so many passages of merit---though the topics are often but lightly treated---so many scenes depicted of Indian interest, and references to the India of history, so many well-drawn episodes of social and everyday life, so many obscure phenomena described and coruscations of thought exhibited, so many vivid pictures and narratives combining the realism of art with the idealism of poetry, that we find it not an easy matter to furnish a specimen of Mr. Mookerjee's skill and ingenuity as a writer, a traveller, or a thinker. As an instance, however, typical of his descriptive powers, we will let him describe the "British Private" as he saw him seated under the "Mammoth Pavilion" of the railway terminus at Sealdah :---

....

We would invite the reader's personal attention to this book, for such descriptions of the Megna and Megna Sea and its tributaries, the fish famine, the last days at Agartala, or the Ripon ovation at Calcutta. With this bare indication of a few leading subjects we leave it to the reader to make his choice of the readable sketches of these travels. Our review would scarcely be serviceable if it did not record the fact that Mr. Mookerjee's unpretending efforts in the contribution he has made to English literature win for him that fame to which he is fully entitled as a man of letters, competent to enlighten his countrymen, as well as those who may consult him, either as a friend or as one who has something of interest to tell them. —*The Indian Spectator*, October 23, 1887.

In that delightful book of his, Mookerjee's "Travels in Bengal."—*The Mahratta*. October 30, 1887.

The spell is at last broken; and Dr. Sambhu Chunder Mookerjee has given us a faithful picture of that littleknown region which separates the metropolitan districts from our North Eastern Frontier, and of the Native State known as Hill, or Independent Tipperah, which serves as a buffer between our territories and the congeries of wild tribes known as Lushais. Dr. Mookerjee is the *Doyen* of the native press; and his first essay in the literary craft dates as far back as the Indian Mutiny. Nor is he wanting in practical acquaintance with his theme; for he paid four visits to Tipperah between 1877 and 1874, and was for nearly two [six] years Chief Adviser to the Maharaja..

....

Our author, Indian of the Indians as he is, acknowledges the undying obligation under which the parent State has laid his country : "It is necessary," he writes, "to keep the best men and the best races straight . . But this insane jealousy of the whiteman I can never sympathize with : It is neither patriotic nor candid. It is simply ignorant and puerile. A moment's inward glance at the source of our most energizing ideas, the slightest enquiry into the derivation of our physical enjoyments---of what we eat, or drink, or wear, or sleep in, or write with, the houses we live in, the furniture we use---ought to be sufficient to disabuse every honest Indian of this unfortunate prejudice." Happy would it be for the dominant race and happier still for its great dependency if all Dr. Mookerjee's countrymen who aspire to form public opinion were actuated by such sentiments as these.---F. H. Skrine, c. s., in the *National Magazine* for October, 1887.

Dr. S. C. Mookerjee, the editor of what is undoubtedly one of the ablest papers in the country in point of literary power, is the author of a pleasant little book of Travels in East Bengal................

The author is master of a racy style of English which many an Englishman may envy. Humourous description and caustic satire enliven every page. There is throughout a vigour and freshness of style that lends a charm to the veriest commonplace. If there were, however, a higher purpose in the publication of his book than to lighten the weary evening hours of the ordinary reader, we confess to a feeling that the author has failed in such an object. We are afraid there is not poetry enough in us to body forth in imagination the beauty of the scenes which the author has described in his voyages to and fro between Dacca and Tipperah. Humourist as he is Dr. Mookerjee will remind us of the words of the poet that the point of a "jest lies more in the ear of him that hears it than in the tongue of him that utters it." As with the jest so is it with the description. We do not say that the charge is unfounded. Prosaic as we are, drudging away at the desk, perhaps it is that we lack capacity to follow in imagination what the author has doubtless delineated with an admirable pen.

One of the chief impressions that a reader will

receive from a glance at the book is the somewhat strained relation between the Babus and the Anglo-Indians. The author pours a flood of ridicule upon the lordly airs of our "rulers." He hits hard indeed in his account of the Colonel at whist enduring a Baboo looking on, when on board the steamer, and of the whiteman's condescension in bowing to the black nigger. Happily we in the South are not so badly off in our commerce with the representatives of Western civilization. In spite of several instances of conflict and misunderstanding Englishmen and Hindus pull on agreeably together. But the author, notwithstanding his involuntary feeling of aloofness from the European, is no stranger to the blessings for which the West has laid us in debt. He has a keen appreciation of the enjoyments of this Westernized life of ours. He looks for ever forward and casts no longing lingering look behind at the things with which we have shaken hands and parted. His heart is in the continuance of British supremacy in the East. And agitation is his utmost weapon for the maintenance of his rights. But he will have nothing with spurious agitation. We extract below a paragraph of excellent advice to his brethren of the press.

....

The author recounts his adventure with the Railway officials of Sealdah with considerable humour. We feel an irresistible temptation to quote it *in extenso*, but space forbids. How the greenback was no legal tender, why silver of the Calcutta mint was wanted and how the currency question stood stiff and frowning despite the Editors and magistrates who had accompanied the author to bid him good-bye at the station, and how again with the advent of the Justice of the Peace all objection to receiving the currency-note vanished, are all narrated in a style that is fittingly characterized only by the word "delightful." In another place the author introduces the reader to the Hindu belief in the auspicious hour for starting on a journey in language of such playful raillery that we make no apology for quoting it. [Extract.]

The untoward circumstance of the day, the event to which we have already alluded, namely the refusal of the Railway officials to receive the currency-note in payment of the fare, elicits the following humourous confession of human weakness. [Extract.]

The author has some trenchant criticism on the isolation of the Englishman, which makes him inaccessible to the complaints of extortion or plunder by their menials. They are too absorbed to know all that passes about them and the wrongs that are committed in their names are unnoticed as mere trifles for they have rarely any idea of their magnitude. It is only too well known throughout the country how blackmail in the shape of money or provisions is levied upon the inhabitants when the Collector is on tour. It would be difficult to believe the thing could go on under his very nose without his connivance if we did not know his exclusiveness and his distaste for mixing with the people.

The author devotes the greater part of the book to a description of the people and the external aspect of the country that he passed through in his two trips to Tipperah from Calcutta and back. He has a good deal to say about the customs of some of the people he becomes acquainted with. He makes a discovery of the debris of a Portuguese Colony in Tipperah that has become debased in morality and sunk in superstition. Although there is not much in the book that is instructive to the serious student, the grace of diction and the ease of style carry the reader pleasantly through. It would be difficult to rescue such a subject as he has chosen from dulness without his extraordinary command of language. We cannot promise more than a brief span of life to the book. It will prove what is abundantly clear to the readers of the *Reis and Rayyet* that the author is an adept in English composition. He is a lover of nature and he paints scenes and situations with an artist's pencil.—*The Hindu*, Nov. 7, 1887.

......this interesting book. We are justified in so terming it, not on account of any romantic adventures that the author has to relate, nor of any very new discoveries in geography or natural history. There is something particular as regards ethnology ; and a great deal of human nature in the book, shown to the reader with a simplicity and candour which bear testimony to its truth. Called from the busy haunts of men in the city to dwell for a time in Independent Tipperah as a judicious adviser to its chief, Doctor Mookerjee relates his adventures during the several journies to and fro in that capacity, without revealing the secrets of the State, like a good diplomatist. He has adhered strictly to the advice which he offers to his brethren of the Native press, and has written what he saw and knows, without revealing all, considering what he might properly say and what withhold....... The above seems to be a curious passage to be found in a book of travels, and appears to have no connection with the subject. But it arises from a casual reference to a slaughter house, and a writer who "thundered weekly against the outrage of locating shambles in the immediate vicinity of a Hindoo temple"—where, in fact, no temple could be said to exist. Hence, the doctor advises his fellow-scribes not to be Pharisees, righteous over much, but to look and be sure of their facts. In the same spirit, he has written his book. He gives an account of his travels, which seem often to have been voyages, upon the wide-spreading rivers of Eastern Bengal which in the rains become almost inland seas. On these he philosophises on the nature of the country and the people, making careful observation of his facts; and though he sometimes fancies he knows better than his boatmen, and more than suspects that they are getting the better of him, he submits with a grace that would have done credit to Socrates, and accepts the apparently inevitable in the interests of peace. The doctor is a close observer of nature, animate and inanimate, with an eye to the picturesque as well as to the sublime and beautiful. And although there is a vein of cynicism running through many of his observations, it is tempered by such evident good nature, that even a stranger would conceive him to be a laughter-loving rather than a stern philosopher. This is evident in his description of his boatmen and others, while he denounces the lawlessness which has made the poor fishermen suspicious even of honest intentions, because they have so long been the helpless victims of marauders stronger than themselves. Their only defence is flight or deceit, and the latter is their justification as a mode of self-protection. We are shown not only the weakness of the people, but the shortcomings of the administration that leave these things possible............ The author is impartial in his censures................. There is much in the book to which space forbids us to refer. That it is not a prosy one may be gathered from the fact that, for its 300 pages, there are nearly as many index references. Many of the subjects are necessarily but lightly treated, but all sensibly and fairly. And Dr. Mookerjee is such a master of the English language that in the whole book we have scarcely found a phrase that might not have been written by an Englishman "to the manor born." There is nothing in it at which any one could reason ably take offence; and there is much from which both Englishmen and natives may learn greatly-needed lessons.—*The Indian Daily News*, Nov. 22, 1887.

TRAVELS IN BENGAL. Such is the title of a most interesting little work published a short time ago. Its author is Baboo Sambhu Chunder Mookerjee the well-known Editor of the *Reis and Rayyet*, the most original, cleverly-written and interesting journal in India. Baboo Sambhu Chunder is one of the veteran Indian writers in English. He is the master of a most happy, racy pleasant style, which you can easily make out from amongst the writings of a hundred different men. In racy humorous writing Baboo Sambhu Chunder has no rival among his Indian contemporaries. He won his first laurels, we believe, by his writings in his own periodical, the *Mookerjee's Magazine*, now long-defunct. In this magazine articles of great learning and excellence appeared, mostly from the pen of Baboo Sambhu Chunder. He has written several other booklets. His *Causes of the Mutiny*; *Mr. Wilson, Lord Canning and the Income Tax*; the *Career of an Indian Princess, Her Highness the late Secundra Begum of Bhopal*; and the *Prince in India and to India* are publications which attracted considerable notice. His production "Travels in Bengal" is a work of great merit. It is at once a most faithful and interesting picture of natural scenery and life in Bengal, although Mr. Mookerjee does not profess to write a picture of Bengal life and uses his pencil in its portraiture only in passing. The dedication is characteristic. [Extract.]

The "Travels" are travels in East Bengal, travels and voyages between Calcutta and Indepedent Tipperah. We do not believe many people in this side of India know that there is such an independent State as Tipperah. But nevertheless such a state exists. We will give here a summary of its history in the words of Mr. Mookerjee. He writes :—[Extract.] Mr. Mookerjee was Dewan of Independent Tipperah for some five years in all between 1877 and 1881. The Travels are an account of his voyages to and from Tipperah.

Those who have travelled in Bengal, particularly in its Eastern districts, which are the districts described in Mookerjee's book, will bear him out in his statement that Lower Bengal is not stale, flat and unprofitable, that, on the contrary, she is the beautifullest country in the world. She has no high mountains, but she has rivers apparently as vast as the sea, to make her scenery grand and majestic. She has a hundred rivers ever overflowing with water, thousands of transparent lakes covered with the lily and a hundred beautiful water-flowers, thousands of seas of ever-waving paddy fields, thousands of clusters of bamboo and of great trees dressed in beautiful creepers adorning the river banks, to make her the loveliest country in the world. Even a Bengali needs to see and travel Bengal to adequately know her thousand witching charms. For a foreigner it is well nigh impossible to get even an approximate idea of what they are like from description, however true and faithful. Let us hear what our author has to say on the subject. We read :—[Extract.] A paddy sea is thus inimitably described :—[Extract.]

We will quote a passage of another character :—[Extract.]

We could cull many such gems. But space forbids it. We will, however, quote some passages of another kind. Our traveller, though old in years, is evidently young in heart, for no one in the romantic age of youth could be more appreciative of female charms than our traveller. In every other page you find our author describing in terms of enthusiasm some rural girl or woman of beauty. [Extract.] In the next page we find our traveller's attention [Extract.]

There is the description, physical and moral, of a Colonel, which we cannot resist the temptation of reproducing, although the article has already exceeded the usual length. [Extract.]

We have now given extracts enough to show that the little book of travels is most delightful reading. It contains graphic descriptions of natural scenery, faithful portraiture of men and manners, and happy, good humoured observations on them. There is not an ill-natured or unkind word in the whole book—it overflows in every page with the milk of human kindness. Every observation testifies to the author being a keen observer of men and things, as an example of which we can mention the instructive and interesting chapter on the Native Christians of Portuguese extraction in Tipperah. Again, although the book does not pretend to deal with life in Bengal, the glimpses of that life we find in it are very considerable and pleasant. We will now conclude by recommending the book to all who may wish to spend a few hours amidst happy thoughts and pleasant pictures.

S. K. C.

— *The Tribune*, Nov. 26, 1887.

If we have not before noticed Mr. Sambhu C. Mookerjee's *Travels in Bengal*, which was published some months ago, it is not because the little book is either dull or pointless. It contains, on the contrary, much interesting matter, though some of the incidents are over-weighted with detail in what is facetiously called a "little booklet." The author's view as a rule is, by the way, facetious: he is given even to punning; but he is also sentimental in the highest degree---"a naked Whiteman" hurts his susceptibilities; a Hindu girl, bathing in the river, throws him into an ecstasy of delight: "she had such large languishing eyes!" But he is nothing if not philosophical, and his reflections on this or that social and political subject are not without their moral. Mr. Sambhu C. Mookerjee was formerly

Minister to the "last of the Nawabs Nazim of Bengal, Behar and Orissa" and afterwards Minister of the Maharaja of Tipperah. He is a man, therefore, of experience, and when he speaks his brethren should listen to him......................................

Travels in Bengal is a readable book, and it abounds in anecdotes which are often as instructive as amusing, and it is not spoiled by too many political allusions, though, of course, some few have crept in.---*The Pioneer*, Dec., 1887.